Memory

Manifesto

Also by Christopher G. Moore

Novels in the Vincent Calvino crime fiction series

Spirit House o *Asia Hand* o *Zero Hour in Phnom Penh*
Comfort Zone o *The Big Weird* o *Cold Hit*
Minor Wife o *Pattaya 24/7* o *The Risk of Infidelity Index*
Paying Back Jack o *The Corruptionist* o *9 Gold Bullets*
Missing in Rangoon o *The Marriage Tree*
Crackdown o *Jumpers*

Other novels

A Killing Smile o *A Bewitching Smile* o *A Haunting Smile*
His Lordship's Arsenal o *Tokyo Joe* o *Red Sky Falling*
God of Darkness o *Chairs* o *Waiting for the Lady*
Gambling on Magic o *The Wisdom of Beer*

Non-fiction

Heart Talk o *The Vincent Calvino Reader's Guide*
The Cultural Detective o *Faking It in Bangkok*
Fear and Loathing in Bangkok o *The Age of Dis-Consent*

Anthologies

Bangkok Noir o *Phnom Penh Noir*
The Orwell Brigade

Memory

Manifesto

A Walking Meditation Through Cambodia

CHRISTOPHER G. MOORE

Heaven Lake Press

Distributed in Thailand by:
Asia Document Bureau Ltd.
P.O. Box 1029
Nana Post Office
Bangkok 10112 Thailand
Fax: (662) 260-4578
Web site: http://www.heavenlakepress.com
email: editorial@heavenlakepress.com

First published in Thailand
by Heaven Lake Press, an imprint
of Asia Document Bureau Ltd.

Heaven Lake Press paperback edition 2017

Jacket design: K. Jiamsomboon
Author's portrait: Peter Klashorst © 2015

ISBN 978-616-7503-35-6

For Luciano Prantera and William Wait

A man sets out to draw the world. As the years go by, he peoples a space with images of provinces, kingdoms, mountains, bays, ships, islands, fishes, rooms, instruments, stars, horses, and individuals. A short time before he dies, he discovers that the patient labyrinth of lines traces the lineaments of his own face. —Jorge Luis Borges

ONE

Cities and countries, their names, shapes, histories, languages, and people—all leave traces behind. There is danger in decoding their mysterious footprints in the sands of time, especially when some of the footprints are your own. My personal mandala contains a space called Cambodia: a circle ringed with other circles designating other spaces with names like Bangkok, Rangoon, and Saigon. The world contains innumerable mental constructions of Phnom Penh and Cambodia. In Borges's infinite library, the memories of the activities, events, and personalities of these places are scattered inside infinite imaginary volumes, each of them footnoting other imaginary volumes. This memoir, like all *memento mori*, attempts to rise out of the category of being another obscure footnote pulled from one of those volumes.

Memories are built from the ashes of old fires from the past. That is the nature of remembered experience—imagining a fire from the ashes left behind. The hardest part is re-creating those flames that once shaped our imagination and feelings. Those ashes, when we examine them carefully, often collapse in a heap. Like buildings, mountains, civilizations, reputations, and cities, memories decay over time until the flame is truly extinguished.

Writers of memoirs are like ancient cartographers, drawing maps before space was rationalized through the invention of compasses and latitude and longitude. Early seafarers, lacking modern tools, navigated by mental maps as they gazed at stars in the night sky. Ashes, fires, stars—these metaphors come to mind when drafting a map of memory. It is said that the devil is in the details. I contend that the devil is in what we have forgotten or misremembered, which is almost everything. Most of us recognize the shapes of the continents and can pinpoint the locations of many countries and cities. As I reach the limits of what I remember, my memory map runs into the flashing sign that says "There be dragons." When pressed, I can only venture into a terrain drawn by doubt and uncertainty.

Be careful when you talk about the past, memory, and intelligence. Do you remember who won the Nobel Prize for Literature twenty years ago? Or do you remember who won the Oscar for Best Supporting Actor that same year? Chances are you'd have to Google to find the answer. Think of where you were two decades ago today. It wasn't that long ago. You were somewhere doing something when the news of those two events entered your life. The Oscars and Nobel Prizes that year, as in the following years, were publicized around the world through broadcasts, newspapers, and magazines.

But if once-famous events of that year have now slipped from your memory, what about the events of your own personal history? The problem with events on that level is you can't Google them to fill in the blanks.

Place, time, memory: these are the three entanglements that define what we experience, remember, and forget. The competition for memory between the scientific tradition and the sacred tradition is one of the conflicts rattling the cage of today's *Homo sapiens*. With only so much memory to go around, what's an ape supposed to do? It is useful to distinguish between the "how question" of memory and the "why question" of remembering. The demarcation marks the fault line that runs between science and political science emerges.

You learn a great deal about people by observing what type of memories they habitually log in to as reference points in their personal timelines—"That was the year I heard live rounds from a AK-47 in a city," or "That was the year I walked inside T-3 prison in Phnom Penh." You learn even more when you investigate why some memories are favored over others for long-term retention. Most people favor one of two types of memory. Story-tellers' stock in trade is the mining of the first type: episodic memory. We love to share our *personal* experiences and those related by others. Story-telling is mainly experienced as a subjective anecdotal experience, one that can have powerful effects to confirm people's beliefs and opinions. Someone tells us a great story, and the next thing we know, we're generalizing the anecdotal experience as if it has statistical validity. It does not. It is a story. We risk a serious error of judgment when we allow anecdotal evidence to override statistical evidence. We read scary stories about inner-city crime and jump to the conclusion that our lives are on the line if we go there.

Today we are experiencing a transformation of culture, society, economics, and politics as millions of people find the official narratives no longer convincing and out of desperation fall back on personal stories as sources of truth. Ronald Reagan drank heavily from the episodic memory well. Today his political descendant, Donald Trump, is an example of someone almost trapped inside his episodic memory. For those who favor episodic memory, simple stories seem to dissolve the knotty problems of a complex world.

Then there are the brainy nerds who recite facts, figures, formulas, and equations in support of a concept or policy. Their attention is drawn to examining a body of knowledge found in books, research papers, government reports and statistics, and vast databases. None of it is directly experienced. This is the interior of another memory silo—the semantic memory.

Those who are prone to tap their semantic memory are the ones who can tell you the capital of every European country, can recite chunks of dialogue from *The Big Lebowski* word for word, and have memorized the names for every muscle in the body and the sugar content of a hundred different foods. They dine on statistics and the names of dead emperors.

Those who win TV quiz shows requiring a wide general knowledge have a highly developed semantic memory. It is easy to impress others if you have a good semantic memory; it is also much easier to avoid any emotions or personal disclosures about yourself. Semantic memory can be socially distancing; you don't feel warm and fuzzy toward someone who has just informed you that 476 CE was the year Rome fell.

Inside our brains both types of memory are at work; you switch between them automatically without missing a beat. In fact the two memory types aren't separate channels but feed off each other. That said, if you place less value on episodic memory, you likely are less interested in novels than in history or science books. Some of us zig and zag. I go through stages of reading half a dozen novels, and then half a dozen books on politics, history, sociology, psychology, quantum physics, neuroscience, or biology. Ask me a year later what I remember about a precise detail in any of those books and I will likely reward you with an embarrassed silence.

A memory palace is a technique for remembering large numbers of objects, faces, numbers, or ideas by mentally situating them in a familiar physical space. The mandala is another kind of memory palace with gateways and layers of symbols. Throughout our lives each of us, whether we are aware of it or not, constructs such a microcosm of our universe. Artists are also mandala builders. They curate society's shared memory palace, transforming the people and places of their time into art. In the tradition of a mandala, this text is a meditation. The center of this mandala you see before you is Cambodia. There is also a tradition in some quarters to make a mandala of sand. I like that medium as a powerful metaphor, but a mandala made of sand would have been difficult to share. Instead I've made mine with words, images, experiences, and thought experiences, marking the gates as I go along.

Cambodia is the main frame I've chosen through which to examine this book's central questions: how do societies tell the stories they tell, and who gets to tell them? To understand the answers we'll need to consider how our memories, on a personal and collective basis, encode, store, and retrieve those stories. Above all we must ask why we remember some stories and forget others. That is a question to keep in mind as we embark on a memory journey through the killing fields.

In the novel *1984* George Orwell scripted the words for a Party interrogator named O'Brien, who explains to Winston, a torture victim, the meanings of history and memory in a successful tyranny:

> All the confessions that are uttered here are true. We make them true. And above all we do not allow the dead to rise up against us. You must stop imagining that posterity will vindicate

you, Winston. Posterity will never hear of you.
You will be lifted clean out from the stream of
history. We shall turn you into gas and pour
you into the stratosphere. Nothing will remain
of you, not a name in a register, not a memory
in a living brain. You will be annihilated in the
past as well as in the future. You will never
have existed.

In this book I explore questions about the forces of
memory annihilation. Who were (and are) they? How did
they gain authority? What have their bankrupt ideologies,
broken dreams and failed social experiments left behind?
The meaning of absolute power over others is that you
may use whatever means available to destroy, eradicate,
erase—the checklist of deletes is never satisfied—the
whole lot of existing memories and replace them with
your chosen memory content. That impulse to power has
always represented the greatest threat to human freedom
and liberty. In the Middle Ages torture and executions
were adequate for the purpose of memory control. Today,
in our post-fact, fake-news era, some memory dictators are
pouring gasoline on facts and reality and setting them afire.
As in Orwell's time, the fear is that the current political
and social system can no longer defend against the memory
dictatorship assault. New technologies are making torture
unnecessary for memory work. The new tools allow for
memory tampering far beyond the imagination of the
Khmer Rouge generation.

Pol Pot's genocide was a serious incursion into the
collective memory with the goal of annihilating it, not
through torture or propaganda, but through mass murder.
His model for memory control can be traced back to
Orwell's O'Brien, who in turn was modeled on Stalin. The

great Soviet dictator had the turn of mind that wishes to create the one complete, absolute symbolic mandala for all of humankind. Pol Pot, like all tyrants, aspired to make himself the god at the center of the mandala and to hold control of all gateways to the center.

The Cambodian Year Zero was the starting point of a memory reset. As a witness to the history of that memory war, I've been chasing after the memory ghosts of Cambodia for a long time. I have sought to understand both the 'how' and the 'why' of the Khmer Rouge, to use Orwell's phrase, attempt to lift Cambodia "clean out from the stream of history."

TWO

A Venus flytrap, *Dionaea muscipula*, is a carnivorous plant native to a tiny patch of ancient subtropical forest. It stays alive and experiences its world by catching ants, small beetles, grasshoppers, spiders, slugs, and sow bugs. As a writer, I find an affinity with this bug-consuming plant. This flesh-eater is a processor of strangers that stumble into its trap. Writers know this game. They play it every day of their working lives as they position themselves inside a cultural forest and wait.

For years I've been trapping my own and other people's experiences, mixing them with concepts, ideas, and facts and digesting them until they've become the words and images of a couple of dozen novels and hundreds of essays. I've discovered there is a certain skill to capturing an event as a plant captures an insect and converting its flesh and bones into a story. I tell myself that the juicy morsel I've trapped represents an insight into the larger ecology and history of the forest, as well as its connection with the world beyond the forest. Readers who want to venture into this forest trust writers to be their forward scouts.

I've played that role for nearly thirty years in Southeast Asia. As an experienced scout, I have a few warnings about my stories and about memory.

Only a small part of my direct experience of Cambodia has been encoded into long-term memory, and how accurate that transmitted memory is depends on how well tuned my senses of sight, touch, smell, and sound were at the time they were employed. Not everything I paid attention to in Cambodia became a vivid memory stored and accessible to me at a later time. Even the best Venus flytrap can't remember every bug it ate. Its experience of the forest, like mine of Cambodia, consists of a succession of seemingly random events that nevertheless, together, forms a regular pattern.

What is lucky for the Venus flytrap is unlucky for the insect, and the reverse is also true. Insects sometimes beat the odds and escape. I face a barrier of how far I can push my memories about Cambodia before invention changes them into things I merely believe, which may not be exactly what happened at the time. The trapper and the trap define each other; that's the story of the cycle of life. This book is an exploration of that life and death cycle in one country.

Reviewing my experiences of Cambodia over a couple of decades, I detected an evolution in a better understanding of the ecology of the social, political, and cultural forest both within that country and beyond its borders. I've learned lessons from experience, and I wish to share with you now the events that shaped that evolution. I'm no expert on the culture, language, attitudes, or ethnic histories of the people of Cambodia. What I offer are observations about a place in a short period of time after a national trauma, in this case a genocide we call the killing fields. The consequences of the genocide carried out by the Khmer Rouge have flowed forward like an underground river, silent and powerful, and sometimes that river still emerges at the surface.

All travelers find some foreign places and experiences more memorable than others. For me Cambodia is such a place, filled with memories that stretch over decades. As I write this book, I ask myself a key question: how much of any consequence do I remember from firsthand experience of Cambodia, and how much am I recalling from the writing, movies, anecdotes, and news reports of others? No doubt my memories sometimes overlap theirs, while others who were witness to the same events will have different recollections. That is to be expected. Lawyers who do criminal defense work know this territory well. The phenomenon of an event being encoded in the memory of one person and not that of another witnessing the same thing has spawned a number of theories. But the fact is that when it comes to memory, much remains a mystery. How and why do we preserve some memories while letting others slip into oblivion? How much of the process of acquiring and storing memory has changed with the rise of the Internet? And how disruptive is that new digital storage system to deeply remembering lived experience?

To write this book, I have accessed the memory vault where I've stored a file labeled "Cambodia" and found there not just genocide but Hollywood, war, cannabis, terror, book launches, refugees, Oscars, returnees, Bill Clinton and Monica Lewinsky, rap poetry, landmines, an anthology I edited titled *Phnom Penh Noir*, and warlords. I meant to pull out one file, and yet it was as if the entire filing cabinet spilled its contents across the floor with tales and experiences from 1993 onward that I hadn't revisited for years. One reason people like to relive the past through their memories is it's a place of enchantment and mystery, with the annoying, boring, and inconvenient scenes edited out. These edited memories are us, and yet at another glance they stand apart from us. The partners in the memory dance are past imaginings and a present longing to remember. Memory also contains a dark, noir component for some; such a memory acts as a pain and suffering journal—physical and psychological pain that is inescapable, disabling, demoralizing and, for a lucky few, an ennobling, transcendent experience. Those lucky ones, wounded but escaped from the Venus flytrap, weave that pain into a revised meaning of life.

I made many trips in between 1993 and the present time. Lately I've tried to reconstruct from memory those people and events that left their mark on me. Memory isn't the actual experience of the world but rather an act of the imagination; it is an imaginary reconstruction of a world that has passed, as if it were still real. As I do my imagining, I'll ask you to believe these imaginings are based in reality, that they happened in the real, physical world largely as I describe them to you. In between imaginings, I'll interject some of the basic science of memory. As this manifesto is partly addressed to the deep future, I'll also be asking the central metaphysical question concerning memory: does memory have any real, physical meaning in the universe, specifically what is the nature of the process we call imagination that links us to our sense of self, supplying the means to find purpose and meaning?

To recall events twenty-five years ago in any detail can only be described as a feat of the imagination. Most of what we sense, feel, or imagine enters and then immediately exits from our consciousness like the millions of massless neutrinos passing through our bodies every second. Memory isn't one thing. We have false memories, incomplete memories, cultural memories, and memories formed from contemporary biases and private and public propaganda. It all mixes in our brains to make us who we are. On occasion our memory crashes. We forget someone or something from the past. When my word-processing software crashes, I lose everything I haven't backed up. We think our memory belongs only to us as only we can access it at will, in a personal, unique way. That is an illusion that becomes obvious when we see how memories are formed and lost. We have far less control over our memory than most of us care to admit.

THREE

Among the powerful forces of nature we are subject to are the chemical processes and electromagnetic charges associated with the memory system in our brains. We have theories of the materialistic basis of memory in the brain, but the fact is we know very little about how memory is constructed, stored, and accessed. It depends in part on the kind of memory. As we'll see, there's more than one way we remember, and different parts of the brain are involved in each way. The memory that Bangkok is the capital of Thailand, for instance, is stored in a different part of the brain from the memory of how to ride a bicycle or climb a tree. In fact a number of memory systems work together to give us the impression of each single, undivided memory so our brains can function smoothly and seamlessly, create a vivid sampling of the complex feedback loops of connected systems that we interpret as the "world."

The fragility of our past thoughts and words, the things we did, and the things that were done to us isn't something we directly feel. The memory doesn't feel as delicate as a snowflake, but it is. Our personal memories may seem to us like physical artifacts of our authentic experiences, souvenirs from that time that have always been there and always will be. The idea that they could be dissolved—melted down by disease or accident, or simply eroded by time—is horrifying. We have no choice but to fight against the Lovecraft's glimpse of a cosmos so vast in space and time that it is incomprehensible, and we are reduced along with our memories to no more significance than the atoms composing our bodies. Anyone who entered Douglas Adam's Total Perspective Vortex machine was exposed to the entire universe with an arrow pointing "You Are Here." No one except Zaphod Beeeblebrox had ever survived the overwhelming sense of worthlessness.

Memory has many types of limitation. And the more we discover about our limited cognitive capabilities, the more we recoil from the horrifying conclusion that, not only are we largely conned by others, but in reality an inner con artist stares back at us in the mirror. What we experience is always incomplete. Something is left out. And when the experience is converted to memory, the experience is further degraded. The more times I recall a memory, the more likely the act of recollection itself will affect the content and accuracy of what I remember. We may reel from the knowledge that all memories are incomplete, unreliable maps, riddled with historical and contemporary biases, and subject to manipulation by powerful official and commercial acts. But more dizzying still is the understanding that this highly flawed mechanism is all that anchors us to reality. We are hardwired to believe that we are like Zaphod Beeeblebrox Douglas Adams' *The Restaurant At The End Of The Universe* and have a handle on the reality of our condition.

We must also contend with false memories that scramble our ability to make sense of our experience and the world. As I write this memoir, I am aware of the dark shadows of incompleteness and false memory. On the positive side, memory as an imperfect truth-catchment system is the only means available to understand the events from our past, including the actions and decisions of those who were in positions of power, and to provide a perspective on the meaning of our own lives and times.

There is a vast literature on how memory can be and has been altered to achieve political and social ends. My favorite memory killer from history is Theodosius I, the Roman emperor who made a notable career out of destroying non-Christian temples and shrines, and burned books that challenged the faith. The period 381–395 CE of Western history is a memory erasure moment that teaches an important lesson, namely that with enough violence and coercion it is possible for a society to regress to a state of ignorance. We know it today because it's been done before. The Roman reign of terror was a war against the memory stored in texts and other artifacts. Eighteen centuries later, the Khmer Rouge waged a war against the knowledge warehoused in the minds of Cambodians.

I am writing these words in my present moment. I'm using a blue pen with blue ink, a gift from my American friend Charlie, who buys them for me in Japan. I am making notes in a notebook that I carry with me. What you are reading is the revised, edited, polished version of those notes at some distance from this moment of transcription. And this moment itself is a recollection of events, faces, activities, and ideas that chase after me like a pack of mad dogs on a narrow path. Currently I am holding my own in running ahead of the pack and hope that I can lose them around the next corner.

We meet in this chosen place: inside a book. That seems an odd, strange "place" as it exists outside geography and outside any joint experience of time. And yet we share a hyper-dimension, as vividly and emotionally engaged as if we sat across a table from each other talking. Of course this "conversation" is one-way. It is also stripped of the parallel communication of facial and vocal expression and body language, the elements that fill out real-life conversations. Another significant characteristic of the literary conversation is that there are no lapses into silence. For the reader the words continue to run across the page without pause.

The selective nature of memory, the deceptions that bend memories, and the identity that is formed from fabricated memories are best described through stories. "Reunion," a novella I wrote for my story included in the anthology *Phnom Penh* Noir (and later published separately), ends with this passage:

> As you get older you find all kinds of ways to leave behind a city, the past, a relationship, a brush with death. This leaving and returning is how life treats us. Equally. If we listen. If we reason. If we find enough whiskey or other triggers to open the sluice gate of truth to wash out the lies buried in memory, we return to a different past from the one we've lived with all of these years.
>
> Phnom Penh brings back that giddy feeling of falling in love. When you're young, the romance of discovery gives you courage. Over time we lose those feelings to the gravity of life. The weight of old losses, grudges, hurts, and betrayals pulls us to the earth, as if they'd been waiting for the right time to take us to a bridge where the giddy romance of a water festival would turn into death. We learn our lessons the hard way. Or we don't learn them at all. Nothing brings back the dead. Not money, not justice, not prayer. Peace is that temporary space where the killing finds a lull. Cover

enough wars and you conclude that coming to terms with past war crimes isn't a contest between justice and peace; it's the dead zone between what happened and what people tell each other happened.

One of the story-teller's closely guarded secrets is that while for the reader the story may come to a satisfying end, for the writer it merely pauses before continuing down a private memory road. When I reread my past writings on Cambodia such as "Reunion" or my private-eye novel set there, *Zero Hour in Phnom Penh*, I think about all of the other stories of Cambodia that I could have told. Cambodia has never let go of my imagination, and each time I've returned to that country new stories have emerged to find their place in my memory. This book picks up where "Reunion" left off, in the memory fields of Cambodia, that dead zone where over time I repeatedly found myself searching for tombstones marking what was buried underneath. I remember what I saw, felt, and experienced there and the reactions of others. These episodic memories are encoded and stored in my autobiographical memory. The other kind of memory I bring to this manifesto, my semantic memory, is the sum of ideas, facts, and common knowledge I've taken from school, books, newspapers, TV, friends, and family. These sources aren't unique to me. Anyone can expand that kind of memory easily by going online. This is the type of memory that is augmented so readily by modern devices. Most people treasure their autobiographical memory the most, but it's our weakness, too, when we're tempted to put too much faith in anecdotal stories. Statistical analyses can be converted into charts and graphs showing trends, probabilities, and error margins, whether accurate or not, but we prefer the story of someone who witnessed the blood and guts.

It seems to us that we have almost infinite semantic memory to draw on. In many ways that belief is a deception. While everyone now has access to more information about China and Russia than any Cold War intelligence agency, we haven't expanded our brain's processing speed. If I attempted to take it all in, my limited mental resources would be overwhelmed.

We have a processing problem that almost no one talks about or wishes to confront. We can only encode, store, and retrieve so much information and, compared with supercomputers, we are as slow as a manual typewriter with a couple of sticky keys. We crunch information, which includes personal memories, at the slow rate of sixty bits per second. You can go on the Internet and find sites promising hacks to increase your processing speed. What they neglect to tell you in those advertisements is that our brains have a strictly enforced speed limit. Like the speed of light, our processing speed has a built-in cap that prevents our going any faster. We marvel at the promise of artificial intelligence residing on millions of different nodes. Such intelligence also has a speed limit but like that of a rocket rather than the horse and carriage of our human brains. The reality of this difference transforms mind travel. We suffer under a handicap that makes our comprehension of reality closer to that of a Venus flytrap.

The most advanced supercomputer stores about four times as many quadrillion bytes as the human brain. Our bragging rights, though, as well as our sense of specialness, survive this realization when one looks at the energy costs of this storage. We use about 20 watts of electricity while the supercomputer gorges down 9.9 million watts for its quadrupled capacity (according to the 2011 *Scientific American* article "Humans versus Brains" by Mark Fischetti).

In time the wattage will likely drastically drop for

machines. As with the old gas-guzzling cars, an engineering and design solution is on the horizon. The same thing is in the cards for an explosion of additional computer memory expansion, opening up an insurmountable gap between the storage capacity of our individual brains and an intelligence system with no individual brain that needs to survive and fears death. Machine intelligence isn't delimited by a small, bony container. Our processing ability has walked at the same speed throughout our 200,000-year history as a species.

I have written this memory manifesto in part for a time in the future when this intelligence capacity and processing explosion will have ended the competition between artificial intelligence and human intelligence. Our white flag won't seem like a defeat to many. Our surrender of memory superiority will be sold as a victory. Hadn't we always feared death, and didn't that fear drive us to make crazy affiliations with religious and ideological constructs that promised transcendence and deliverance?

Secular deliverance will come when the first of our kind has successfully uploaded her full memory into a silicone-based information system. How and where that upload will be stored has the potential to create a mini-industry of panels, conferences, reports, recommendations, and TV pilots. These are the obvious traditional methods to respond to change, though in this case they may be too slow and irrelevant. It is possible that soon after our personal information is harvested down to the finest detail of childhood memory—every face, sound, touch, color, and smell will be stored and preserved—someone will find a way not just to upload, to *uplift*, his memory but to tap into the system's processing speed potential. Not long after those two events follow one another, there will be an uplift of intellectual activity that makes our present-day concept of memory meaningless.

When we reach that point in our history, the meaning of memory will have fundamentally changed. It will no longer be atomized, individualized, and we will wonder that personal identity was once defined—really trapped and distorted—by the limited processing speed of the species. In those days it really didn't matter that information exploded beyond the capacity to store all of it. All that mattered was everyone was in the same boat: locked in a skull, with limited processing speed, and what separated the genius from the fool was a slightly more efficient oar.

After this book comes out, there will be other memory manifestos. The new genre will work as field guides to surviving inside the Total Perspective Vortex machine and promise an alternative to religion or ideology. Such works will represent the naïve belief that after the uplift that is coming, books will be used to post-facto bring back the memory of the author. That would be an insane use of resources. But though scarcity and competition have constrained and limited our range of actions up to now, if the future brings a new abundance, then why not experiment with a reconstruction exercise from a memory manifesto, to see to what extent the information in a book was a blueprint of the author's memory, and how that memory was linked to and shared by others?

FOUR

It wasn't that long ago that my episodic and semantic memories worked together and unwittingly blinded me in ways I couldn't understand. For most of my life I have relied on photographs and other people's memories of shared events, mixed in with gossip I've heard, films and videos I've seen, newspaper articles I've read, and personal notes. This treasure trove of memory was, so I thought, unique to me. Don't we suffer from the common delusion that somehow we are special, unique? And yet the age we've come to occupy has produced new aids that suggest otherwise. Amazon and Netflix, for instance, remember my ordering history and have no trouble recommending books or movies or series that its algorithms often correctly suggest are consistent with my values, reading taste, and literary interests. Every whorl of our digital fingerprints adds more information to identify who we are, what we like, our friends, our political affiliations, nationality, geographic location, martial status, education, age and entertainment preferences.

Our tastes, desires, and prejudices are collected, stored and sold to corporations seeking to market products and willing to pay for better sources of information to predict our buying behavior. Elementary but powerful AI systems track us. And if you wear a Fitbit, they track your sleep patterns, too. Our memory is being encoded offline (offline from our brains) in hundreds of ways. We are unconscious of how each keystroke creates a memory trace in a digital brain, one that already knows better than you do what book or film you will "like." Each time you buy a recommended book, film, iPad, sofa, chair, shirt or watch that purchase is logged into digital memory. Your digital golem is alive and living inside cyberspace. That golem of you is cloned by its new owner and sent back to you as a piece of your own memory of liking. Every time you log on, your doppelgänger awaits to greet you with something to please you and that you will like.

Our digital memory guardians look after us as if we were residents in the wing of an old people's home reserved for those with damaged memories. You might argue that our semantic and episodic memories are being curated, enhanced, and expanded, and that we have nothing to fear and everything to gain. We are simply buying books based on previous books we liked or renting films that we might otherwise have missed. We rely on our memory guardians which monitor our every like and consumption choices. We assemble our reality through battalions of algorithms networked in the brain; the network allows us the ability not only to process the present but also to construct a model the past and predict a future model. Our cognitive abilities evolved to allow us to escape the fate of other animals—being virtual prisoners of instinct caught in the present moment. But our reconstruction of the past is often incomplete, flawed, biased, or irrational. Memory suffers from fragments appearing to be the pieces of the whole puzzle. We forget. Even when we remember, it is only partially what happened and even that is dependent on time and place. Perhaps for the new generation nothing of past interest will be forgotten, and the contextual limitations of time and place can be overcome. They will be reminded of what they liked even if they've forgotten why they ever liked it. We are suckers for nostalgia, and refreshing an old, pleasant memory ranks as a kind of pleasure few would forgo.

But as technology advances, we may rediscover the value of forgetting. Up to now our great fear as a species has been that the record of our lives will be erased upon death through whitewashing, a memory extinction. In the future, our fear will be different. The center of our primal fear may shift as we enter a universe where nothing is ever forgotten and can be accessed at any time. We may revise our thinking and wonder how much freedom is lost when we can no longer forget. It's not always a bad thing to forget. We stigmatize forgetting as evil. But is that true in every case? Isn't part of being human our capacity to forget?

Our minds are noisy places buzzing with voices, smells, sights and sensations, feeding our fantasies, fears, desires and dreams from the coal-fired engines deep inside our unconsciousness. We have a subjective sense that these things belong to us; they are our secret, private domain, a sanctuary we can retreat to. The ideas of 'private,' 'belong,' and 'sanctuary' collapse once our digital golem takes up residences in thousands of spaces trolling for objects and services in a never-ending search for happiness, pleasure and meaning.

Our golem speeds through H.P. Lovecraft's vast empty void of the universe like the engineer driving our ghost bullet train long after our physical death. It leaves a comet like trail of countless boxcars cramped with our lifetime of stories— the ones we've heard, the ones we've told, and the ones created in our head. All those stories, translated in all human and machine languages, past, present and future, in perpetual rearrangement, like a casino dealer shifting millions of decks of our accumulated information, photographs, dogs, cats, food, likes and preferences. This is not the immortality we wished for but our longings and wishes are as transitory as our mortal memories. All those stories wallpaper our memory palace encasing us in a tomb. They leave more questions than answers. But there is nothing wrong with that state of affairs. José Saramago saw the kind of question you ask lays naked your intentions. He said, "Your questions are false if you already know the answer."

This is the time and place to ask questions about Cambodia to which I don't know the answer.

FIVE

Phnom Penh. January 2017. Street 136. Tonle Sap River. That is a memory tag giving my time and place in Cambodia earlier this year. My previous trip to Phnom Penh occurred a couple of months earlier. Here I was, after a short time, back again. I'd come to its river to remember, much as I once would go to the Spanish Beach in Vancouver, a place where I could find things in my memory as if a river or bay might open a memory tributary.

My friend, ex-New Yorker, John Fengler booked me a room at the Lux Hotel on Street 136, actually a huge suite with old Soviet-style furnishings. The hotel was near the river. All I had to do was cross the Sisowath Quay and walk along the Tonle Sap, and the magic of remembering carried me along like a strong current.

Turning from the Sisowath Quay onto Street 136 placed the river at my back, the setting sun in my eyes. The street, it seemed to me, hated sunlight. It was a nocturnal beast that lured its nightly prey into the heart of darkness. After dark, entertainment businesses with names like Candy Bar, the Red Fox, 69 Bar, and Tiger, with hostesses sitting outside under neon signs, lined the main thoroughfare and side streets. I've experienced bars as places to forget rather than to remember—not that, for many of us, forgetting through alcohol is such a bad option. The problem is when forgetting becomes the default setting, and what is left behind over time is a memory so thin, so distorted and confused, that it takes a lot of alcohol to live with it.

On this last Cambodian trip I found some clarification about a number of questions I had as to why this city functioned for me as a memory storage locker. The plan was to go to Cambodia, open that locker, pull out a memory I hadn't thought about in a long time and smile, thinking, yeah, I remember that time and place; I remember what it meant to the people of Cambodia, how it was the end of an era. Then I would consider how it represented the peak of my power to process the raw experience of a place that history had visited with genocide, mass theft and destruction, and pandemic madness.

Infamous T-3 Prison Phnom Penh 1993

It was 1993, when I was in the country to cover the period of the United Nations Transitional Authority in Cambodia, universally known as UNTAC. Fighting with the Khmer Rouge continued along the border with Thailand. People were still getting killed, though the numbers were comparatively small. Members of the press, all 2,300 of them had been accredited by UNTAC officials. I was just another brick in the wall. Where were these thousands? I never saw more than forty or fifty at press briefings.

Two UNTAC soldiers, police officers from Ireland and Malaysia, took me under their wing and guided me through various offices and down back streets. I conspired with them to sweet-talk the Cambodian prison guards at T-3 Prison, a notorious French-built prison that has since been torn down, using the time-honored currency of Johnnie Walker purchased at the UNTAC PX. That bottle opened up the gates that led us to the main grounds, where we found women in hammocks dying of tuberculosis.

T-3 Prison women prisoners Phnom Penh 1993

We continued through the main courtyard, which looked more like a refugee camp than a prison, where sick women, elderly men, and children were left in the open to die. Our guards chatted as if we were strolling through a museum exhibition. I could tell by the way they looked at the people on the ground that they didn't see what I saw. They had scored their bottle of whiskey. It made them happy, proud, and confident. We were led into a chamber lined with steel doors with small, barred windows through which we could look into concrete cells, deep, long, dark places. The guardian unlocked one of the doors and we stepped inside. About two-dozen young Khmer men, no more than teenagers, looked up. Dressed in shorts, shirtless and shoeless, they had dead expressions, the kind you see on people who have lost all hope. They said they were sitting waiting for their ankles to be shackled to the concrete floor. We'd interrupted the procedure. The door opened and I was allowed to take photographs. With my Canadian passport and shiny press card, I was an alien from a different world where free men could magically appear and disappear from a dungeon.

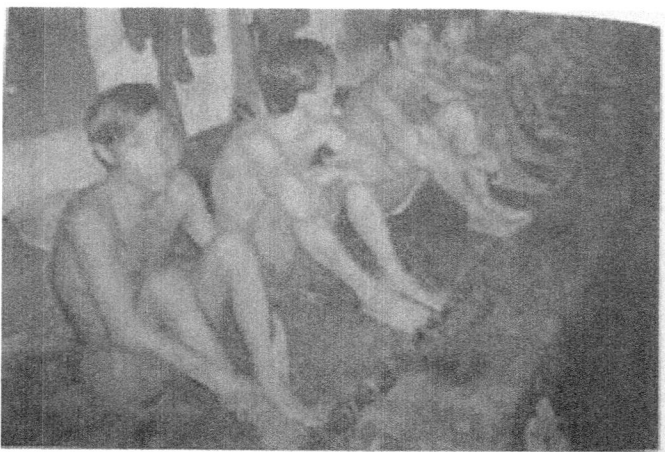

T-3 Prison prisoners Phnom Penh 1993

I pulled out a small film camera—there were no smart-phone cameras back then—and snapped photographs of the prisoners and the conditions of their confinement. These photographs eventually appeared along with a story I wrote for the September 1993 edition of a Malaysian law journal.

The day after I went on the unauthorized tour of T-3, I stopped by the office of a UN official and told him I had taken photos that I would send him once I had developed them in Bangkok. The official, who was about my age, also came from Canada. Common nationality cut no ice. He refused the offer, and he couldn't wait to get me out of his office. He'd been to T-3 earlier that week and had been assured no one was shackled. He didn't remember anything like what I described having seen, images of misery and suffering that my memory wouldn't let go.

After I had the film developed in a shop on Sukhumvit Road near Soi 27 where I lived, I sent them to a big agency in New York City called Magna. Some American crisis erupted and the editors pushed the story with my photos of the shackled Cambodian men off the page. No one cared. The world wouldn't remember them. The cover of the original 1994 edition of *Zero Hour in Phnom Penh* (then titled *Cut Out*) featured my photo of a young Cambodian utterly defeated as he stared out through steel bars. Neither he nor the men I'd seen shackled in T-3 would be lodged into our collective memory. They were lost lives thrown into the pit of oblivion.

I had found myself in the office of a gaslighting UN official. He denied what I had witnessed. The gaslighter's stock in trade is making you question what you've seen until you doubt your own sanity and question reality itself. It was an old trick: establish a thumbnail of doubt about my story. I'd made him unhappy. I stood a chance of ruining his day. Journalists often cause cognitive dissonance with their uncomfortable stories. I'd dragged my eyewitness testimony like prison chains into his office. A UN official tells you that you didn't see anyone shackled, and a news agency can't sell your photographic evidence because an America-oriented story was chosen by editors to enter the public memory instead.

I realized in 1993 that I was part of the modern process by which collective memory was encoded, stored, and transmitted, but also that others had to co-operate with sharing the information or the memory would be lost. I learned that not everything a journalist finds is "newsworthy." Then and in the years since the UNTAC period in Cambodia, opinion on the importance of events or activities of that time was necessarily limited by what was recorded and passed on. My experience was that this information-gathering process was uneven and incomplete. In the early 1990s I learned a valuable lesson about Cambodia, people with power, and the limits of what could be shown and told. Once I had faced off against a UN human rights official whose job was supposedly to protect the weak and vulnerable, I knew that my eyewitness accounts, my press card, and my nationality meant nothing to the gatekeepers who truly had the power to change things.

I learned that people will ignore the evidence of what you have witnessed because to acknowledge it might mean the end of the road for their career, their beliefs, and their network of contacts. Instead I was the one at the end of a road. My contribution to the collective memory was as significant as the life of one Venus flytrap to the overall health of the forest. The public memory of my images and accounts of prisoner abuse died from lack of replication. A private memory could be contained, isolated, extinguished. I was humbled. I left Cambodia with a different understanding of the people who lived there and the international representatives who had gone there to oversee a transition to a lasting peace. I had learned the hard way that forgetting was an unofficial part of the peace process.

At that time I had no alternative means of publishing my account. If I'd had access to the online media of today, I'd have posted the photos on a blog, Facebook, Instagram, or Twitter. The UN official would have soon found himself in hot water. My photographs would have entered the memories of many others. But in 1993, when my photos of shackled prisoners in T-3 weren't published in a major media outlet, the result was a deletion from public memory. It was like a bullet in the neck in the raging bull of truth.

You might be thinking that not everything can be remembered, and that is true. We all want others to be aware of what we believe should be part of the public memory. We compete for the attention that is needed to preserve a memory. Before the Internet, journalists had to persuade their editors or agents of the importance of their stories and photographs. Now the competition is with cat, dog, and food photos, and funny videos of politicians. Have we progressed in the memory retention sphere? You can see arguments on both sides. When everyone becomes a story-teller, the balance is tipped against semantic memory. And that is a real and present danger.

In Phnom Penh in 1993, my story and pictures had to audition along with miles of stacked stories and photographs before an overworked editor. It wasn't as bad as finding a publisher for a book, but my 1990s experience in journalism convinced me that over the great span of history, most stories and visual representations predating photography have been lost. The archeology of memory is much like that of the scientific evidence for the origins of our species. We construct elaborate stories from a few bones, tools, and cave wall paintings, and these serve as portals to thoughts, desires, drives, conditioning, and relationships. We want the past to share its memories with us in the present. The problem is that what the past delivers is shorn of most of its wool. The wool we can gather amounts to just a few threads, from which we must reconstruct the tapestry as best we can. We accept this impoverished, incomplete replica as the full, rich reality of the past.

Cambodia during the UNTAC period was like being at the bedside of someone who'd been pulled out of serious car crash—so many international troops and so many walking wounded, mingling together. Remembering that time now is not unlike trying to recall what it was like moving around a city before electric lights and cars. Phnom Penh was a dangerous hellhole. I heard gunfire most nights. I sat on the balcony of the Lido, staring through the rails, as bullets whizzed down the street from a checkpoint, and the street girls and their customers dropped to the ground, though I never saw anyone hit by a bullet that night. The experience of reality on any evening in Phnom Penh in the early 1990s was shaped by factors of light, time, transportation, carelessness, and stupidity, and I don't want to leave out the pull that comes from the capacity to inflict punishment on those who oppose you. If you have an AK-47 in such a place, you are a kind of god. The point is that I experienced firsthand a ruined city, a people emerging from a period of devastating war and genocide, and an international UN peacekeeping force with police and soldiers from around the world having the time of their life in the midst of all that misery.

My early memories of Cambodia were created before the time of social media timelines. No one born in the last thirteen years since Facebook came online will have lived in a space untainted by timeline memories. There is a growing gap between them and those of us whose episodic memory once came primarily from direct experience of the world, a kind of living that has now largely vanished except in the most desperate parts of our planet. Somewhere along the line we've conflated our timeline experience with actual experiences. In the new memory century, we've encoded digital flows of information as if they were actually happening to us. Our brains and memories have been rewired. Our experience-processing brain no longer recognizes any essential difference between what we saw on the street and what we saw on the screen. The two converge in our brains. Slowly our memory has become integrated into a computer-generated river of information, symbols, images, and sounds. Analog information-gathering falls into the same category as using flashlights at night. It's slow, and you'll have to put on your shoes and venture beyond the comforts of home, but if you want any diversity in your episodic memory, you'll have to take a long walk into the world.

We don't experience darkness as our ancestors did. Our sense of darkness is logged in memory, but that memory is difficult to access across decades of no direct knowledge. What separates us from our ancestors into a different fear zone isn't the absence of the sun (electric lights chased away our instinctive fear of darkness). There is something that technology hasn't been able to fix, namely, the darkness within our species. Artificial light doesn't reach that place. But you can catch a glimpse if you look closely enough. I saw that darkness in the T-3 Prison courtyard with dying women in hammocks, glossy-eyed, staring into nothingness and doomed to die behind prison walls.

In 2017, looking at the shoreline of Phnom Penh from a riverboat on the Tonle Sap, I found another perspective on the city. Floating on a boat, you see the land and the people there in ways that evade you when you are on solid ground. Most of my other memories of Cambodia are of noisy and dusty streets, alleys, buildings, slums, and markets—all the crumpling infrastructure of a place that I'd digested in small pieces. I was too close to take it all in. Phnom Penh was changing from a city where time had been reset to zero. It revealed itself more like a palimpsest with the old scraped away and the new painted over. Coming across an older layer, our memory marvels. That is the nature of memory. We are always surprising ourselves by finding what is underneath. I wanted to read all the overwritten histories and experience all the events that had been recorded. Instead, I was confined to my own time and experience, winging back to places like the Lido, the UNTAC PX, the command buildings, the machine-gun emplacements, the news briefings, and the T-3 Prison as I saw it in my off-the-books visit. These places physically had disappeared and all that remained was the memory of what had been.

From the riverboat I had the illusion of taking in the whole city at one glance, reading each layer of the palimpsest.

Something for your semantic memory: the Tonle Sap is a river and also a great lake. The combined river and lake system is 250 kilometers long and 100 kilometers at its greatest width. Remarkably shallow and fat, its depth averages one meter with a maximum depth of ten meters. The subject of myth and fable and the historical center of Cambodian transport, agriculture, and trade along with smuggling, raids, and piracy, the Tonle Sap was one of those random, accidental events etched into Earth's geological face. Eons ago the Eurasian Plate and Indian Plates smashed into each other, leaving a large depression. Water filled the depression and produced the conditions for the formation of a great lake whose dimensions shift enormously between the rainy and dry seasons.

I boarded a five-dollar tour boat on the Tonle Sap at 5:00 p.m. The cruise lasted an hour. A couple of dozen people sat on plastic chairs scattered across the top deck and alongside the railing to watch the sun set and snap photographs with their cellphones. Two young women from Hong Kong took selfies, and a group of three young Cambodian women did the same. Several elderly couples looked at the setting sun in silence. A young couple sat close together, sniffing each other the way young lovers do in Southeast Asia, as if the sun were glowing beautifully just for them, to celebrate their romance. In years to come, will either of them remember that moment? I wonder.

I had first come to Southeast Asia, specifically to Bangkok, to write a novel. My arrival there at the end of 1988 coincided with the closing years of our analog memory age. I had no idea at the time that I was about to step across a threshold that would change the way we remember. I stayed on like a lodger who was given a room, watching the others who came and went at the expat boarding house. They will remember those times. Everyone has favorite memories of the past. One memory was a life-changing question. I'd been drinking a beer on a beach in Phuket with my friend Ronald Lieberman, who asked me, "Why hasn't anyone ever set a private-eye series in a place like Southeast Asia?"

SIX

No writer could have asked for a better mentor than Barney Rosset. He found me through my Vincent Calvino books, about an expat private eye in Bangkok, and sought me out. From the early 1990s until his death in 2012, I listened to Barney in Bangkok or New York City talk about his war years in China, his relationships with Henry Miller and Samuel Beckett, his time in Havana with Dick Seavers (editor, translator and publisher), his exploits defending freedom of speech in the American legal system, and his bitter fights with Ann Getty, who had bought Grove Press. Over the years, I wrote the occasional essay for Grove Press's Evergreen Review. I was listed on the masthead as its Bangkok correspondent.

Many events shape a life. War shaped Barney's life and left an impression of the world that he carried with him ever after. He talked about his time as a young officer in the American army assigned to be an official filmmaker in China. Years later, with the help of Bob Bergin, arrangements were made to show Barney's wartime photographs in an exhibition in Kunming.

We met in Bangkok—Nana Plaza, Patpong, the Thermae, and various dives that passed for restaurants in those days along Soi 23, Sukhumvit Road. My wife and I visited Barney and Astrid at their loft in the East Village.

They threw a party for us and invited various literary types and publishers. Larry, their landlord, was a fan of the Calvino series and asked me to sign several books for him.

Barney Rosset with Christopher G. More
National Book Award 2008 NYC

The last time I saw Barney was at the National Book Awards gala dinner held in the Financial District of New York. Barney had asked me to look over his speech beforehand, and I offered a couple of suggestions.

In 2012 Astrid phoned me from New York and told me that Barney had died on the operating table. He'd gone under the knife for heart surgery. He was eighty-nine years old.

The old businesses and personalities of Soi 23 from Barney's days in Bangkok are gone. I thought of him the other day when, crossing the road, I came face to face once again with a small outdoor watch repair shop outside an old-fashioned barbershop. It was like coming upon a stagecoach repair depot. The old watchmaker still repairs watches as he has done for the last thirty years at that spot. As it happens, his shop is across from the original location of the Old Dutch restaurant, where Barney and I once sat on the upper floor eating rice. My memory of that meal is conflated with those of many other meals with Barney. I never saw him eat. The meal was always bagged and he took it back to his room. His hand always clutched a glass of rum and coke, which he nursed. At the end of the meal he always had a waiter or waitress bag his food and would carry the bag back to his hotel or his loft. Astrid once assured me that over a number of days he would work his way through the contents of the bag.

Barney Rosset at the Old Dutch Restaurant Soi 23 Sukhumvit Road Bangkok 1992

Leftovers and rum and coke kept Barney alive for eighty-nine years, so I wouldn't scoff at his eating and drinking habits. A good mentor teaches you how to eat, how to choose what to do with your life. Eventually he also teaches you how to die. But it's Barney's relationship with food that stands out for me at this moment. Dinners and lunches in New York and Bangkok were always the same—Barney seated in front of uneaten plates of fried rice, pasta, beef, and potatoes, clutching a drink. I wonder now whether he used his approach to dining as a sort of hypnotist's watch, a stage device to capture and hold attention.

The instruments we use to "tell time" and to measure it have changed radically in a generation. Those changes have been as great as the shift from the water clock, which the ancient Romans and Chinese used, to mechanical clocks with levers and gears and pendulums. At one time a Roman family's status was signaled by the type of water clock in its villa. The Rolex watch recently served the same status function, though the new generation no longer wears watches but simply checks the time on the screens of their devices. The status timepiece bird has left the cage.

For most of our history time was divided between day and night. Like most other animals we rose with the sun and retired as darkness arrived. Our ancestors had no conception of hours, minutes, and seconds. Those are modern ideas, ones that were harnessed to drive the industrial and scientific revolution. In the time of water clocks there was no uniform standard time. It shifted within cities and between cities, and no one ever thought being punctual was a virtue. We don't think twice about the importance of timeliness. Like cleanliness, it is automatically assumed to be good and tardiness wrong, bad, and sin while not venal it is close. In Thailand and Cambodia most of the locals rarely suffered under the yoke of this particular virtue. It wasn't uncommon for the different sense of time drove newly arrived expats into madness and despair. A few years ago, I wrote an essay titled *Noon and Midnight: Time in Thailand*. That essay proved to be one of the most popular of hundreds of essays I've written. People seem to pay attention to how others move around the world as if they are lost time travelers.

Watch repair shop soi 23 Sukhumvit Road 2017

The watch repairman's shop is an anchor memory for me of early 1990s Bangkok in the shadow of Soi Cowboy, a place where a lot of people spent time. It was a quarter of a century later that I passed him again, still sitting on his stool behind the glass case with secondhand timepieces, a jeweler's loupe positioned over his right eyeball, staring at the mechanics of timekeeping. As I look now through the loupe of time at the picture of Barney and me at the original Old Dutch restaurant, I try to recall the memory of that dinner, that conversation, the heat, the women, and the dreams, and I think of how the slide show that runs inside the human mind is a series of interlocked, selective, and unreliable little nodules of memory, slippery as eels and as trustworthy as a politician running for election.

The watch repairman had spent his life working on similar timepieces that tick-tocked with tiny, circulating three-fingered hands, each finger moving at its own speed, each pointing at us to remember what comes next and what happened before. Sundials, water clocks, clocks made of candles and incense... There have always been clock inventors, watchmakers, and watch repairers, and then there are the rest of us, lost in time, trying to remember what happened.

SEVEN

My memories of Cambodia, Thailand, Vietnam, and Burma (Myanmar, as its government now refers to it) are a jumble of puzzle pieces of varying sizes, shapes, colors, faces, smells, gestures, voices, choices, events, dangers, missed appointments, close calls, relationships, deaths, births, divorces, graduations, and a fairy dust of feelings that have accumulated much as a snowstorm buries mountains. When I try to assemble these pieces into a coherent picture, I am left with the unsettling feeling that something is missing or something has been added. Time is a brutal editor of memory, and the older you become, the more that brutality hits home.

A memory manifesto of my time necessarily privileges direct, personal experience—the episodic memory—as the gold standard. (Trump's campaign embodied a memory war: the semantic memory experts against the episodic story-tellers. Now that he is in office, the war continues, its final outcome uncertain. A great deal of our future depends on the eventual winner.) What we store from our own experiences, we can draw upon when we adjust our identity, forge allegiances, or seek to avoid danger or find pleasure. In these memories we retain our lessons about the nature of the world of men and women. Our brain is a memory library. Retrievability from the memory shelf is imperfect. We never remember most of what we experience and ultimately forget most of what we do briefly remember. Try to remember what you had for lunch the second Friday of last month. Or describe the clothing, height, weight, and age of a person seated next to you on the bus or train two days ago. In reality, we screen out of our episodic memory much more than we save. As hard as we may try, we just don't gain much ground in remembering.

The mind is a busy place, like the hub of Heathrow Airport, with many flights arriving and taking off every minute of every twenty-four hours. You sit in the departure lounge clutching a malleable, leaky roller bag with your nametag on it. Inside is your memory. It's packed with not just your own memories but those borrowed from other people so long ago that you're no longer fully aware that they're second-hand artifacts, hand-me-downs. If someone were to ask you right now if you packed your own bag, after some thought you'd have to admit you're not sure. That realization should make anyone suspicious. Asked which memories are based on genuine experiences and which result from second-hand experiences told to us by others, we can't completely distinguish between the two. As far as our memories are concerned, like a Venus flytrap we assume everything we swallow belongs only to us.

Should catastrophe strike, the loss of the contents of that memory carry-on will result in the existential loss of the building blocks that have made you who you are. Oliver Sacks wrote a number of books and articles about people whose memories had been lost, damaged, or compromised through injury, disease, or genetic flaws. *The Man Who Mistook His Wife for a Hat* graphically showed through case histories what happens to people's sense of self when they lose the ability to recall their past. The mental life of patients who can't remember becomes an uncomfortable reminder that there is no substitute for the memory-based self once memory is fully lost. The illusion of a concrete, distinct, and individual self rests on vulnerable, unreliable, incomplete constructs manufactured from images and emotions without the aid of a truth filter. Subjectivity personalizes our memory. Sacks expressed the process of human memory this way: "There is no way by which the events of the world can be directly transmitted or recorded in our brains; they are experienced and constructed in a highly subjective way, which is different in every individual to begin with, and differently reinterpreted or re-experienced whenever they are recollected."

We are memory magpies building our memory nests from found parts, and generally we are not concerned with whether any particular experience happened to us or to others. Memories have no record of provenance attached, through which we can trace their original ownership. We assume in most cases that we are the original owners of our entire memory.

We are also born mind-travelers. Everyone has a gold card for frequent memory traveling. When we find ourselves stuck in the terminal in what passes for the present, our attention is mostly elsewhere, either in the past or in the future. We are rarely present in the moment, mindful of a time and space that is here and now. Our attention is constantly diverted by public announcements, advertisements, commands, warnings, delays, and boarding information. We are immersed in an environment that constantly reminds us that we must soon be somewhere else, like the passengers told to report to a gate or perhaps summoned to security. The present, unless you are a meditation practitioner, is a state of mind to leave as quickly as possible.

I write these words in a present that will long have expired as you read my words in your present. But I leave this manifesto as an example of one person's attempt to bust out of the mental airport terminal of the mind. I glance sideways at my pen as I write these words in a notebook, one of the pens mentioned earlier, bought for me in Japan by my friend Charlie. I'm well aware that my scrawled handwriting in this moment I'm seeking to share will disappear into a much fussed-over published text a great distance from here and now. Perhaps you can sense my frustration in this effort to share what is not shareable between a writer and a reader: the moment.

Books create an illusion of shared memory between the author and the reader. This book is about memory and memory trials, traps, obstacles, and blocks. All books are one-sided transfers. Every reader has his or her own book of memories, but generally they're not ones I can buy, borrow, or beg to see. That's the inequality of books; as in a one-sided marriage, only one of the partners speaks. Some people don't read for this reason. They feel like a puppet with the strings of their memory pulled this and that way. I tell you about a friend named Charlie, a pen, a notebook, and you fill in the visuals, sense the mood, and the tug on your own memory banks where you've stored similar experience. That's where we can meet. I'm in the seat beside you in the departure lounge where you've been waiting for a flight. It takes a special kind of effort to pull you away from your plans; in Yiddish its called chutzpah. There is brazen audacity in producing a work that aims to seize control of a reader's mind and feed it hours of the author's own memories. Readers need some very powerful reasons to yield to that memory dump into their brains. Try to remember every book that you've read. How many of them do you remember? Can remember the titles and authors? What was central theme, the revealing detail that changed your opinion or view of yourself or life in one of those books? At the time you were reading, a book may have seemed unforgettable. Ten years later you can't recall even the title or the author's name. It happens to all of us. Only a few books stick in our memory over the long term. All our lives people are seeking our attention, wanting to pull us away from our private mind travels, to urge us to take a flight with them, and curious, we open a book that, as time passes and our attention is diverted elsewhere, we forget like the face of a blind date we never saw again.

I have over a long writing career a novelist's knack of pulling readers into a story to keep them turning the pages. As a lawyer and law professor, I had a knack of pulling together seemingly unrelated patterns and events into a coherent narrative that was plausible even though it wasn't necessarily true. There is a novelist inside every lawyer looking for a way to kick down the door and escape the conventions of objective facts. I believe it is possible to form a better understanding between episodic and semantic memories and the role played by our unconscious brain. Memories are the scripts that little knowing voice announces the reasons to justify that part of our decision-making process that we have no direct access to. I'm telling a story about memory based on research, facts, clinical and medical studies, and case histories. I am modeling reality and the better the model the less surprise I have about encounters with events and people. I am also telling stories that I've personally experienced. I am riding two horses at once by telling two kinds of stories, engaging two distinct kinds of memories, with a single goal: to better understand this memory game that deals me a hand that I read as explaining who I am to myself. My hope is that if this text can reach a deeper, richer understanding of these issues, in the process it may pass along a map or a model you can use in charting the formation of your own memory palace.

EIGHT

At the end of January 2017, one evening I went to Smalls Bar in Bangkok, carrying a copy of my book of essays *Fear and Loathing in Bangkok*. I know the owner, David Jacobson, from the early 1990s in Saigon, where he had opened Q Bar, and I was staying at the hotel next to his bar. During my Vietnam law firm days, I wore a suit and tie and sat in an office waiting for clients. I played that *Waiting for Godot* role from 1990 to 1995. Before Cambodia I'd been among the first Westerners to enter postwar Saigon as Vietnam opened to foreign investment.

After the office closed for the day in Saigon (a.k.a. Ho Chi Minh City), I would head straight to the Q Bar at 7 Lam Son Square, District 1. My hotel was part of the Saigon Opera House, which previously had been the National Assembly. Some nights I'd leave my top-floor room and climb through a small trapdoor that opened to the ceiling above the opera house stage. I'd sit there unseen, watching the performers on the stage and the people in the audience share an evening of entertainment. After the show I would move on to David's Q Bar to report my critical review of the performance. The bar attracted a diverse crowd that had its own stories to share. At the time Q Bar had a growing international reputation as the expat story-telling hangout for journalists, travelers, English teachers, diplomats, writers, and a new wave of young professionals taking advantage of Vietnam's having opened a crack. These were the people who filed through that crack of opportunity and continue their existence to this day in my mind's eye. I sometimes wonder if that secret door above the stage has since been sealed.

In 2017 in Bangkok David celebrated his seventieth birthday with a party at Smalls, his latest bar. He asked me to sign *Fear and Loathing in Bangkok* for him. David led me over to a little alcove with a desk in the corner, where he fumbled around with the dodgy, ancient electrical wiring, looking for the switch to turn on a light. After a minute or so he succeeded, and the location of a pen was magically revealed along the side of the desk. He didn't have a friend like Charlie to constantly bring a fresh supply of pens. David had been a professional photographer in Los Angeles and had photographed many celebrities. In one photo, a very young David pretended to spar with Muhammad Ali, who was at his peak. He left LA to become one of Southeast Asia's most famous bar owners.

Writers need pens. Bar owners need booze and glasses. In the dim light, I signed the book, wishing him a happy birthday. I looked at him for a long moment. I remembered the nights I'd drunk in his Saigon bar. I had a vivid recollection of the night he had explained how a nephew had been commissioned to paint a Caravaggio reproduction on the walls of Q Bar. It was the perfect artwork for postwar Saigon in the early '90s—young, wild, and dangerous. Neither of us realized how young we were then. Since then we'd both grown old; if we'd been buildings, we'd have been covered with thick ivy. He and I had shared a past that had been a defining time for collecting episodic memories. You either experienced the Saigon in the early '90s or you acquired your information from the memories of those who had.

I have a personal memory bridge between Saigon and Phnom Penh. Let's take a stroll over that particular river of time. One afternoon a walk-in client named Larry, an American in his late thirties, arrived without an appointment. My secretary showed him into my office. You learn a lot about clients by looking at their hands. As this stranger, dressed in jeans and a T-shirt, eased himself into a chair, I noticed the grease under his fingernails. His large hands were rough, his knuckles scuffed and raw like those of a workingman. He wasn't the kind who'd feel comfortable in a place like the Q Bar or today at Smalls Bar. Most of my law clients had soft, baby-skinned hands devoid of the telltale grooves, nicks, and cuts that come from working on machinery. Those hands were more accustomed to holding a single-malt whiskey; they'd never taken apart an engine.

Larry told me that he had had his own business in Maine running an auto parts store and had built up a good business. Before that he'd turned nineteen years old while serving in the US army in Vietnam. No matter what he did, whatever success he achieved and whatever adulation he garnered from his friends and neighbors, he couldn't get Vietnam out of his mind and heart. He regretted what he'd done years before as a soldier and so had recently returned to Vietnam with the personal mission of making amends.

"What I want more than anything is to open a second-hand auto parts shop in Vietnam. I'll start with a branch in Saigon and then spread out to other places. Who knows, may be even Hanoi."

I thought for a couple of minutes before I said anything. Larry leaned forward, his hands together in a finger bridge that might have been mistaken for prayer.

"That's not going to work under Vietnamese law," I finally told him.

The Vietnamese were taking baby steps to open up investment and trade. It would be much farther down the road before foreigners who lacked the backing of global corporations could obtain a license to open a second-hand auto parts shop.

The verdict destroyed a long-standing dream and broke his heart. But there was something deeper at work. I'd seen it before in Americans Larry's age who had drifted back to Vietnam looking for something to do or to contribute, and to find work that would allow them to sustain themselves there. Part of the motivation was guilt for their part in the war, but that was only part of it. Their memories of Vietnam were from a tender age in their lives, when most young men are drinking, smoking pot, chasing girls, and going to parties, films, or the beach. Larry and men like him had instead been walking through rice paddies, shooting and getting shot at, seeing buddies killed before their eyes, and sleeping with young local women during their R&R. What had been laid down by their episodic memory in Vietnam had not faded away over the years. Over time it became clear to them that no later experience could ever come close to the power and thunder of their Vietnam days. Larry had come back not only to open a second-hand auto parts shop but to return to the place where those memories had been formed. He wanted once again to be in the place that had supplied him with the most important memories of his life, the ones that had defined him. It was gutting to realize that Saigon neither remembered him nor wanted him.

That was the law business in Vietnam in those early American embargo days. Americans like Larry hadn't been much more than boys coming back to Vietnam on their own. This time around they'd been drafted not by Uncle Sam but by their memories; they'd returned to search for the boy who'd become the man in jungles and rice paddies. War had left a trail of vivid emotions in their minds, ranging from heart-pounding moments of when the bullets rained down to memories of raw, uninhibited sex, and no matter what they did after that, nothing ever came close to matching them. Larry was one of America's—to borrow from Pol Pot—Old People. Since going home, life had been rough for the Old People. Decades later it was still rough enough for them to vote for Trump, who implied he had his own Year Zero plans for America's New People. Over the years I bumped into many men like Larry, Venus flytraps with an acquired taste for a certain type of insect he associated with the process of becoming a man.

That half an hour with Larry in Saigon one afternoon in 1992 returned to me when I arrived in Phnom Penh in 1993. I walked through a memory palace where the rooms were filled by damaged, broken men and women who as children had experienced terror, death, disease, and violence during the time of the Khmer Rouge. Their episodic memories had warped them, making it difficult to adjust to life. Wartime memories played the harmony part of the music that was their lives. The horror of that time was the only tune they could hum by heart. It was also the passport to levels of elevated adrenaline fear, and dread that no soft-handed man or woman of peacetime can grasp.

One moment, Larry was sitting across my desk in Saigon; the next, I was standing at David's tiny desk at Smalls in Bangkok. The year 2017 had flipped into 1992 and back again to 2017. As far as I know, Larry never visited the Q Bar. I don't believe I ever mentioned him to David. But there I was at his birthday party thinking of this character lodged in my distant memory.

In 2017, with a bar crowded with David's well-wishers, there remained a fraction of a moment when David and

I were both squarely in the present time frame. We were friends in a distant past. We knew many of the same people. We had a connection. But that moment came and went. The signed book connected us for a genuine moment, but such moments last for a short time. Our 2017 Bangkok moment ended with an interruption by a member of David's staff, who whispered in his ear. David disappeared from the room and the moment.

People are always disappearing from the moment. They fly off to the past or the future. You can't stop them; you have to just let them go. Wave goodbye. At the bar I saw Nicholas Simon, a filmmaker who'd also experienced Saigon in the old days. I'd been in Saigon throughout the first half of the 1990s, six weeks at a stretch each year, working as a consultant for a law firm during the day and going around the city by night looking at what decades of war had inflicted on the population. Nicholas said he'd been in Saigon from 1994. I didn't know him from those days, but he remembered David's Q Bar from that time. If you don't have a past experience that you share with someone, the next best sharing is a future where a joint memory is being forged. That opportunity came when I bumped into Nicholas Simon.

Nicholas and I talked about the current state of the project of selling the Calvino series as a TV series. We also had a common friend in Milan Popelka, COO of FilmNation, who'd been trying for eight years to put together a feature film deal for the Calvino books. The two of them had joined forces, and it seemed that at long last there was serious interest by a producer/director in Hollywood. The producer/director was putting together a cast list for a TV series. Milan said there would be more news in a week or so but told me not to get my hopes up, not to board that plane to the future, as most such flights end up canceled, and even those that get off the ground are as often as not diverted or aborted or simply crash. That didn't stop Milan from being excited—or Nicholas, or me, from sharing in that excitement. We all wanted to be on that flight, and standing at the bar with a glass of water, talking with Nicholas, we were no longer in the present; we were in the summer, five months ahead, when the deal was done, the money paid, and our plane, arrived safely at its destination, was taxiing to the gate.

I was no longer in the present moment. I was in the future with Milan and Nicholas and Vincent Calvino. I had boarded that plane with two real-life characters, plus one fictional character whom I'd created, imagining a place that didn't exist except in our minds, and soon the plane of the future was airborne. Sandwiched in between a remembered Saigon and a dreamed-of Hollywood, only a fraction of my time was spent in the actual moment of David's birthday.

NINE

Phnom Penh is like a boxer who's been punched, stabbed, stitched up, and thrown back into the ring bleary-eyed, swinging wildly at ghosts of the past. It is beyond our comprehension to process the amount of death, destruction, and misery that was inflicted on the Cambodians. Genocide isn't just another word for mass murder. It attempts to annul the past by killing those whose memories are inconsistent with the murderers' plans for the future. Writers, thinkers, teachers, scholars, journalists, priests, and government officials were all fed into the meat grinder. They were murdered to destroy the past and cancel their role in the future. Year Zero for Pol Pot and the Khmer Rouge demanded the extermination of the "New People" and the delivery to the "Old People" the real Cambodia that had been taken from them. Pol Pot started a trend. Wage war on New People and wipe them out. Afterwards the Old People will worship you as a god.

Memories can be readjusted after such slaughters. The irony was Pol Pot and his close associates were themselves New People, acquiring their political knowledge in Paris—you don't get more New People than a French education on the intellectual basis of political theory.

The point is you change collective memory when you make most of your cognitive workers and intellectuals enemy number one and systematically murder them. Once they are gone, the memory is lost, and you can create the illusion they never existed. Political power has the ability to delete and rewrite our memories, until what actually happened becomes deleted from our knowledge of the past. The Old People can sometimes be led to believe their future will only be secure in the hands of a strong leader with an eye on Year Zero. Once a people's collective link to its accumulated wisdom is severed, the remade people's subjective reading of the world is drawn from *tabula rasa* inscribed with the images, beliefs and ideas of a powerful, charismatic leader.

I believe that no one can be present in their life unless their core memories are drawn from the well of personal experience. I also recognize that limiting your choices and decisions to only what is suggested by personal experience won't work. No matter how varied, exotic, and unusual your range of experience may appear to others, it will never be sufficient to fully prepare you for the complex choices you must make in life, given the complexity of human nature, psychology, and technological and demographic changes, to mention a few. All will have a tangible impact on you. That's why we need people whose semantic memory allows our brains to predict probable outcomes. People will argue which kind of memory has greater predictability—the commonsense approach drawn from episodic memory or the statistical analysis of the probabilities of several different outcomes.

Do you want to model your memory on an ancient forest or a city designed from the mind of a contemporary Baron Haussmann or Le Corbusier? The value put on one kind of memory over the other will influence the architectural style of a city, from density patterns to types of lanes and sewers to governability. In Year Zero, the Old People started from scratch by emptying Phnom Penh, a hive buzzing with New People and their ideas.

TEN

In my room at the Lux Hotel in Phnom Penh, the bed is positioned against a wall with a nightstand on either side. On the right side of the bed, built into the cupboard, is the control panel for the lights. Twin lamps are mounted on the wall above the nightstands. The lamps are positioned for bedtime reading. The standard of a hotel rests on the quality of several co-ordinated activities and services. The ideal guest room is clean, the bed meticulously made, and the bathroom in pristine condition; a room service menu appears predictably on the coffee table, and remote controls for the air-conditioning and TV are easy to locate. The difference between a one-star and five-star hotel isn't confined to the luxury of the lobby, the room fittings, and decorations; it is rooted in the professional care and attention paid to every detail in the room.

Just now I pulled back the nightstand to the left of the bed from the wall, looking for an outlet to recharge my cellphone. It seems as if no member of the cleaning staff has pulled back the nightstand since the start of Year Zero because when I looked behind the nightstand, I found a crumpled-up piece of mauve fabric. What was it? What was it doing there? I pulled it out. It was a polo shirt left in an inside-out condition, as if the owner had been in a headlong rush to undress and flung his polo shirt over his shoulder as he dived into bed. That is a story, a novelist's projection; it's also a plausible explanation. I have no idea how to judge how long the shirt had been behind the nightstand. A layer of dust covers the fabric. I sit on the edge of the bed and stare at the shirt. This kind of accidental discovery has happened to me before. I turn the shirt right side out and its logo catches my attention: Beverly Hills Polo Club. On the sleeve is another logo, with the number 1982.

Polo Club. Phnom Penh. Beverly Hills. The Lux Hotel. I sought to process the connections of between this hotel room and rich people and their horses in California. This isn't the first time something like this has happened to me. For better or worse, I make a habit of finding patterns in disconnected strings of objects, people, or places. Fifteen years ago I was at the checkout at the airport in Rangoon. I'd placed my passport and ticket on the top of a desk. A clerk, who sat dwarfed behind the large wooden Victorian-style piece of furniture, looked up as she examined my ticket.

"Where is your passport?" she asked, looking at me as she waited for an answer.

"I gave it to you with my ticket."

I patted down my pockets just in case.

She shrugged and looked up at me with those cold, official eyes.

"I need your passport."

"But I just gave you my passport."

But that wasn't strictly true—I had put it on the desktop. I likely was drifting into the past or the future and not paying attention. I'd not been fully present.

The uniformed woman behind the desk made the effort to look around, picking up her papers, looking underneath.

"It's not here," she said.

Another official appeared on my left and asked if he could help. I explained the situation. He exchanged a knowing glance with the woman behind the desk. Neither of them believed me. We had a standoff. My passport had gone missing. Now I was stuck in the present. In Rangoon. At the airport. No outward flight for me. I tried to look at the setting to see what I'd missed; normally we miss a lot of what is simply in front of us. Then I saw it. Not the passport but a huge, ancient piece of teak furniture left over from the colonial past. Some elephant had dragged that tree down a jungle trail. Probably it was not the elephant that Orwell shot, but it might have been a close relative. I looked more closely at this Victorian monstrosity and for the first time I saw what had been present all along but I had overlooked. A crack of several centimeters had opened between the large edifice and the workstation behind it.

The official helped me pull the furniture away and inside was a treasure trove of lost keys, sunglasses, wallets, and pouches; my Canadian passport rested face up on top of a camera. I saw the eyes of the official go supernova as the treasure lost over many years was revealed. This was to be his lucky day. It certainly was my lucky day, as I reached into the pile of loot, picked up my passport and a fancy (for the time) camera. I lifted the two items as if they belonged together. If the official had witnessed my deception he pretended not to notice. His eye was on the larger cache of valuables, and the sooner I left, the sooner he could collect the haul. But I had an ethical problem. The camera wasn't mine. I'd not lost it. From the dust, it appeared to have been from another time, and lost to the owner and anyone else. I could have handed it to the official, but what would he do with it? Put in a lost and found? How would the owner ever know the fate of his or her camera?

I slipped the camera with the undeveloped film in my pocket. I'd find another way to contact the owner. Later I wrote a book set in Burma called *Waiting for the Lady*, and this camera appeared as a key element in the story. I used that camera as a literary pulsar sending light in search of that one reader who would have recognized the model number, the airport, the large desk, and the number of pictures recorded.

I never had anyone contact me with a note saying, "That was my camera."

As I looked at the Beverly Hills Polo Club shirt in my room at the Lux, I took that mental flight back in time to Rangoon. I saw myself squatting on the floor, my hand cupped over my passport and the camera. The official stood off to one side. "I found my passport," I said, looking up, and proudly showed him. The two officials couldn't process me fast enough. They'd been motivated for this foreign witness to leave so they could divide up the hidden spoils I'd uncovered. Inside was a history of travelers who like me hadn't been present at a significant moment. Their minds, like mine, had been someplace else just then, as they entered a time and space where things went missing. The effort to remember what happened when we weren't paying attention is doomed to failure. Distraction, it is said, is the enemy of memory; too much input and our minds shutdown; we can't handle the overload and the information isn't properly processed. Our mental system 'hangs' like any other processing system that has exceeded its capacity.

A couple of years ago I wrote an essay about a traveler who had lost the race to enter a Bangkok Skytrain at Asoke Station. The doors had been closing as a young man ran toward them. In a desperate attempt to cheat fate—or perhaps as an offering to the door gods—he had stuck through his hand with a plastic bag containing milk, cereal, yogurt, and a banana. No doubt he meant to use his hand as a wedge. The strategy didn't work. He withdrew his hand at the last instant, leaving the transparent plastic bag dangling from the closed door as the passengers stared at it and at the young Thai man on the platform as the train pulled away with his breakfast.

For writers, these lost objects ignite the imagination and can become a source of inspiration for an essay, a scene in a book, or the theme of a book. Such objects and the experience of finding them worm into our memory. When we are separated from something that belongs to us, we feel a sense of mourning. What had once belonged to us can no longer be found. It's gone with a finality resembling death. Such losses can become raw material for a writer who uses them to invent plausible stories explaining who lost them, what they were doing at the time, what distracted them, and what space their mind occupied at that moment. The circumstances and the objects—a shirt, a camera, a bag of groceries—invite us to imagine human stories of loss, regret, discovery, and meaning. They are reminders of the perils of distraction. They are also a harbinger for the loss of our most valuable possession: our memories. Lost people and things left behind in airports, hotels, or taxis are reminders that even the best minds are stretched to capacity in their efforts to keep track of the people and things in our personal worlds.

The Lux was a no-star hotel. The old airport in Rangoon, unchanged from Orwell's day, was a no-star airport. I'd been passing my days in a series of no-star spaces from another age. The no-star places came from the age when human memory had no assistance or backup from computers. Your memory was pretty much your only means of storing what you experienced, and when that was lost, like the shirt, the camera, or the groceries, a part of you could no longer be retrieved.

Most normal people learn to let go. That isn't a story. It is a state of being where no story is necessary. But my story-telling mind couldn't help but invent the polo shirt's owner as a Hollywood mogul, an A-list producer or director who had gone off the grid to ride the wild, untamed polo fields of Street 136, Phnom Penh, where an experienced rider could choose from a large stable of fillies. The occupant of the room, in my mind, owned a string of polo ponies, employed a personal trainer from Spain, a groomsman from the Philippines, two illegal Mexicans to keep the stables clean, and a coach from England, and his boots and saddle were highly polished. Mr. Beverly Hills sat tall in the saddle as he leaned forward, striking the ball solid. But what had my Hollywood mogul been doing on Street 136? Had he been alone? Why had he left his polo shirt behind the nightstand, or like my passport, had the loss been a random accident? What did he remember now of that room? Did his memory include this lost shirt and events surrounding that night?

In my pre-computer days, I used my memory and imagination to fashion stories. That was nothing knew. My resources were those employed by story-tellers from the dawn of human time, when stories were first told around a burning fire. The difference between the lost-and-found incident in Rangoon and the one in Phnom Penh is the Internet.

I Googled "Beverly Hills Polo Club shirt," anticipating rolling green grounds, a lavish clubhouse, horse stables, beautiful people with glasses of champagne, smiling with perfect teeth and, of course, wearing Beverly Hills Polo Club shirts. That was the story my imagination in the mere seconds it took to do the Googling. Instead, I found the shirt was part of a product line that included sunglasses, scarfs, jackets, bags, belts, watches, and shoes. The product line had a Facebook page in Thailand and showed a Manchester

United player wearing a polo shirt. The probability that the shirt I found belonged to a Hollywood mogul had diminished to the near zero chance of an asteroid hitting the planet this week.

You didn't need to earn millions of dollars to own a Beverly Hills Polo Club shirt. They could be charged on a credit card from $36.00. They were available on eBay. This was an exclusive-sounding brand for a non-exclusive crowd. I'd stumbled upon a singular item that pointed to an explanation of how the capitalist system functioned. Memories had become a commodity you could find new or second-hand for a nominal price. It no longer mattered that you had no memory of the actual polo club in Beverly Hills or had never ridden a horse or even seen a polo match. You could advertise an imaginary association as if it were a memory of ties with an elite class of people and its entertainments. Capitalism had made everyone a spinner of fictional worlds. We shouldn't be surprised to hear today's shout-outs about "fake news" and "alternative facts" as we live in a world of objects and events whose names and labels only fit our reality with a flight of imagination.

Labels and brands no longer reflect the underlying reality of the products they're attached to. Republican, Democrat, Conservative, Liberal, and Labor are among the terms that have been hollowed out and, like the Beverly Hills Polo Club shirt, merely appeal to a human desire for an attachment of the self to a symbol. It no longer matters that the symbol has been diluted. Labels and brands are memory crutches, a kind of consumer Braille that allows us the feeling that we are special. Everyone wants to win the marathon, but no one wants to run that far for a medal. We live from mental shortcut to mental shortcut and let our memories believe that we are runners at the head of the pack.

Our memories were always compromised by the overload or neglect of our perception and the noise that causes incomplete or distorted information storage. That state of affairs is what makes us human. The more expanded the perception, the less the noise, the more we approach other qualities and possibilities, but the truth is that at some point we leave the human realm with its flaws, delusions, and incompleteness. It is inside this larger realm that writers have woven threads that patch over the incompleteness of life. We seek out the perfectly ordered forest without weeds or pests, pretending that such a forest isn't just decorative and that it can be sustained. Outside the realm of fiction, though, we should make space for the weeds, the pests, the poisonous snakes, and the plants that have no commercial use but form part of a healthy ecology. The demands for a neat, tidy memory mirrors the history of our modern cities.

Cities were once unruly, illegible spaces. Then Urban planners and designers like Haussmann and Le Corbusier came along. They sought to quiet and control the noise of space by rationalizing, organizing it into systematic, controllable areas where efficiency and order allowed for the interception of all uncivilized acts and thoughts. Opaque nooks and crannies, narrow, winding side-streets and impenetrable neighborhoods were fertile breeding grounds to hatch plots and spawn terrorists. Architecture served the interest of powerful patrons. Haussmann and Le Corbusier fashioned tools to control and direct the legends down myths the chosen boulevards, tame the rivers, hills and fields, eliminate the slums and untidiness, which provided the scaffolding from rituals and symbols to ensure obedience and loyalty.

Our memories have more potholes than an upcountry road in Cambodia. The rain gets in. We seek shelter in what we remember. We rely on the inventory of memories to explain ourselves to ourselves. We search for meaning and relevance and often find neither. The right brand of polo shirt is one of those shortcuts, the bargain we make with ourselves to stop the fear of not fitting in. We aren't the rider at the polo club; we are the horse, and we have a rider on our back, putting in the spurs. That rider is the opinion of others, their approval, their acceptance of us. Our memories bend to the gravity of others. Anyone willing to drink the water of this truth learns she drinks alone.

ELEVEN

Midway through the Tonle Sap River cruise, the boatman turned slowly toward the shore opposite the city of Phnom Penh. There the flat, green landscape stretched to the horizon, showing little evidence of commercial or office buildings, roads, schools, or modern housing. In such open spaces people's memories are of a different order from what is remembered in places like Phnom Penh. A river can divide not just an approach to visible structures but the people who inhabit them and their ways of seeing things. Not long ago it divided the Old People on one side from the New People on the other. The political and military structure of the Khmer Rouge has since largely dissolved, but the people in the millions who once backed them remain in squalid conditions.

The New People now have a toehold on the green side of the river; from the boat, I could see the beginnings of development had begun to travel inland. Before the boat had turned, someone on the boat—his accent marked him as an American—announced to no one in particular that he'd counted twenty-five construction cranes popping up in the Phnom Penh landscape. That was before the boat faced the opposite side of the river, when he remained silent. There were no construction cranes on this side of the river to count.

One large building complex dominated the skyline as seen from the river. This was the Sokha Hotel, with its five wings fanned out like a poker hand. Big money can scale a building into a majestic symbol. The symmetry of the hotel's interlocking wings presented perfect rows of windows catching the sunlight from the water. Its shade of paint seemed a memory trap waiting to spring. Was its pale yellow a nod to daffodils, buttermilk, shortbread, sugar cookies, bananas, or eggs? In the ballroom a golden color washed the ceilings, the chairs, and the walls. I was on a boat, not in the ballroom. I later saw a photo of the ballroom online. My direct experience had left a memory hole, and like a good road maintenance worker on a potholed highway that stretched for hundreds of miles, some professional photographer had captured the Beverly Hills Polo Club shirt image of opulence, elegance, and splendor. If you wore the shirt into that room, you would be inside a space that made you feel on top of the world. You'd stand in the center of that huge room lined with a king's ransom of gold, catch a reflection of yourself in the polo shirt, and without knowing it, would have taken a flight far away from Phnom Penh. Strapped in your mental seat, you'd have been transported to another place.

My memory of the Sokha Hotel is from the distance of a riverboat deck. Other than its employees, only a handful of ordinary Cambodians would have ventured inside. From the boat, the hotel appeared lifeless, more like a public monument—the Ashmolean Museum, perhaps—than a hotel. The Sokha Hotel was light years from Oxford. But my memory produced a strange association between the two buildings. My memories often surprise me in this fashion. They return to consciousness something I've not thought about for years. That's what makes each person's memories unique: the way they are gathered over time, stored, and accessed.

Not long after the boat sailed past the Sokha Hotel, rows of squatter shacks appeared along the riverbank, like weeds in the hotel's carefully manicured forest. The light caught the tops of corrugated steel roofs. I remembered similar shanties outside Battambang that were situated one hundred meters inside a field of landmines. A small path to the shacks was marked by a bright red danger sign showing a skull and crossbones. One of the deminers walked with me to the tumble-down hovels, where children played in the dirt. The Old People lived with mines. When they moved to live in a riverbank community in Phnom Penh, they recreated from memory what they knew. Their community within sight of the hotel was a reminder that collective memory travels and leaves its calling card in its structures. In the Old People's underworld there were no daffodil-colored walls or polo shirts. This was a community of people separated by the river and clinging to it. The people living on the undeveloped side of the river moved in a world without room service and buffet breakfasts. They lived in a different world with different memories.

The two worlds occupied practically the same geographic area—they existed within sight of each other—yet they remained illegible to one another. Isolated and estranged like different species that drink from the same watering hole, one a predator, the other prey, each occupied a niche that history indicated would expand in favor of the predator. Nature had a balance that bureaucratic states teamed up with profit-seeking predators had destroyed. The riverbank dwellers waited not for construction in their community but its destruction; it was in the cards as they watched the cranes across the river. You might say that the destruction will be a good thing. Isn't it a goal of progress to free people from the misery of slums, their health hazards and drug addictions, and to bulldoze their crime-breeding shantytowns, educate their children, and absorb them into the community of the developed world? You could go on a say that development has already pulled many of the dirt poor out of abject poverty, so stop blowing that horn of hopelessness.

The poor also have memories. They just remember different things. The Old People remembered a different Pol Pot from the one the New People remembered. I doubt any members of the squatter shack communities followed the war crimes trials of the Khmer Rouge leadership. The trials weren't for them; the trials were an attempt to satisfy the New People—especially those in the West—that an attempt was being made to achieve justice. Justice, in the case of the Khmer Rouge, was a New People's obsession. The problem was that trials, justice, and remembering the past from the New People's point of view didn't have much relevance to people inside shantytowns. Nothing had changed in their lives, and they struggled as before. These impoverished communities no longer had political power. They were just a bulldozer and a bank loan away from being even further isolated and scattered. The fact was that neither category of people had absorbed the other over time. Each had clung to its own experiences and memories.

The poor might be agreeable to exchanging their memories for those of a developed, modern, secular world, but we don't live in a world that will willingly finance that transition. The Old People had their Year Zero and the promise of a utopia that proved to be false. As our boat slowly sailed downriver, we passed a number of other riverside slum communities. Like the reeds they sprouted near a source of water. As in a natural forest, the diversity of designs of their shacks showed an ingenuity and individuality that comes from making do with scraps of salvaged or stolen objects such as wood, metal, and screening. None of their buildings had been put up according to a municipal plan, permit, or license. None conformed to urban people's ideas of what a house should look like. The shacks had no blueprints; they sprang from memories of the past.

Slum community on the bank of Toule Sap 2017

When they walked out of their shacks and looked at the Sokha Hotel, what must have gone through their minds? Envy? Hate? Or was it something like admiration or desire, or just resignation? If you'd been dealt that hand in life, rather than the suite in the Sokha Hotel and the designer gear on your back, what memories would you lay down about the daffodil-colored structure rising in the distance and the people who came and went in expensive cars? I don't believe there could be a simple answer to these questions that could lead anywhere but to a confirmation of a bias. We can't free ourselves of the cultural and class biases that act as filing drawers where we store our memories. Our willingness to accept collective memories reinforces the strength of our social relations and our status within a community. That is one reason why the Old People displayed their sense of community differently from the New People living in cities. History is filled with examples of the clash of opposing communities' collective memories. Sometimes in that conflict, compromise no longer works. The memories are too different. A leader emerges who resorts to genocide as the best way forward. If you kill a class or an ethnic or sectarian group, your victory is that their memories die with them. The solution of killing everyone with an alternative set of collective memories has a long, ignoble history.

The New People got their start with printing presses. By 1520 the printing of books started a revolution of ideas that spread across Europe. Suddenly there were thousands of books; literacy was the train the New People rode to a new way of remembering. One result was war. A window for religious wars opened for over a hundred years (1524 to 1648). The Reformation wouldn't have happened without the printing press. The conflict over idea control and orthodoxy resulted in many deaths. A fault line opened between the old orthodoxy and a new class of memories, with new ideas, ones that could be communicated outside official Old People's channels. A New People's memory was forged as the modern technology changed not just how but what we remembered. That change in collective memory started a process of war that runs in a historical line from the early sixteenth century through the Khmer Rouge period.

I am one of those New People, and as you are reading this book, you are also part of that community. I also have respect and time for friends who come from the Old People's side of history. I couldn't have written the kind of novels I have without their friendship and trust. Intellectually, my memory comforts me that the New People's objective description of the world is more accurate. My emotions send me a different message—if I needed someone to watch my back in a war zone, I'd want someone with an Old People's memory of loyalty, sacrifice, and friendship. How does anyone choose one set of memories completely over another?

To be honest, most of what I have stored in memory over a lifetime is unreliable, irrelevant, distorted, incomplete, inaccessible, or infected with one cognitive bias or another. I am not immune to habitually thinking that I have this memory thing under control even when I know that is untrue. No one does or can control it. That doesn't stop me from trying to make intelligible judgments about the world around me, though I stumble and fall each time I think I can run down a dark memory path. I trip over things there that are as delicate as a flower. Or a Venus flytrap.

When I try to stay in the moment, it's not that I slow down; it's that time passes more like ancient time before sundials and water clocks. There is the time of light and the time of darkness, and you adjust your behavior and expectations accordingly. In my mind's eye I can smell the river as I look at the shacks in the distance. I look carefully. I never see a person. It is as if the slums are abandoned. It is 5:30 p.m. and the sun is setting. I wonder if the people who live inside are working and won't be home until late, or if they are unemployed and have no money to leave their shacks.

There never has been a Cambodian welfare system that looked after the needs of the poor. Families and neighbors shared what resources they could spare. The Old People of Cambodia sold their labor for food. The price of food was expensive, the cost of labor cheap. I can imagine some of them returning on the cross-river ferry after a bone-aching workday across the river in Phnom Penh. At night in those shacks, as I recalled from upcountry, the dead stillness of late afternoon would give way to the sounds of music, drinking, shouting, and laughter. It also occurred to me that the shacks themselves would block out the view of the Sokha Hotel. I imagined it didn't oppress them the way I felt it would oppress me if I lived in one of those shacks practically within the shadow of such opulence, the dark shadows of discontent where revolutions are plotted. The shack dwellers occupied their own mental space, and inside their airport terminal, so to speak, past and future evoked the relationship between their community of the present and its collective memories, supplemented by their individual experiences as community members. What seemed to me like life at the bottom of the barrel was the product of my memories and not theirs. Both the Old People and the New People used drugs and alcohol to plug the holes in their memories and avoid thinking too much about questions with no answers.

TWELVE

I stopped drinking in February 2008, a few months after Max Voigt, an old friend from America, died from alcoholism at the age of sixty-seven. Max was a fine corporate lawyer. For many years he lived around the corner from me, in a small cottage within a family compound off Soi 27, Sukhumvit Road. He had the conscience of a social worker. His difficulty was reconciling who he was inside his memories with the work he did. He felt the misery and injustice of the world, and the dissonance tore him apart. Max would drink ten glasses of vodka after work in Nana Plaza so that he could earn the one free drink. After he'd downed the eleventh vodka, he would stumble back to his house and pass out.

He drank like this seven days a week, not because he lived at the bottom of the social barrel but because he lived and labored in a world where legal work was done to take advantage of those who did live at the bottom of the barrel and had no ladders to rise from it. It was his job to protect the rich against other rich, powerful people but also against the underclass of workers that fueled their enterprises.

When Max died in 2007 I told myself I wouldn't end up like him. Six months later I stopped drinking. No twelve-step program, no counseling, no pills or pep talk. Since then I've never once missed alcohol. I am glad, though, that I once drank with the best of them. It taught me a great deal about memory and forgetting. I thought of that drinking time as I sat on a plastic chair on a boat, looking at slums along the riverbank. I'd gone out of the present and into the past as if someone had flicked a light switch. There was Max sitting beside me, eyes red, rattling the ice in his glass as he looked at the shacks. "No one should have to live like that," he said.

"How would you fix it, Max?"

"It can't be fixed. It can only be endured."

"Endurance has an end," I said.

"That's why the poor drink," he said. "To extend the end point. And that's why alcohol is legal. It keeps the lid on."

By his seventh drink Max would start to slur his words, his face would flush, and his blue eyes would go watery. His thoughts would become incoherent, his theories outrageous, and his mood sad and angry. The shacks would have upset him. He would have drunk faster. When you match drinks with your friends, everything slides into incoherence at about the same rate. When you stop drinking, a different reality appears. Max loved playing darts. He'd enter dart tournaments at Domino's on Soi 11. They kept score on a white board. Sometimes Max won; it was one of his few pleasures, winning at darts. But when you drink and throw darts, unexpected things can and do happen. I saw him throw a dart that missed the target and stuck into a nearby calendar on the wall, right over the right breast of the nude model. Max won a free drink with that shot. I remember the way he smiled, sheepish and knowing, as he pulled the dart out of the paper breast.

When you drink with your friends, you hardly notice the change in them because it has overtaken you as well. Each drink acts like a lift going down, stopping each time one floor of coherence below the previous floor. You never stay on any one floor long before a new drink arrives and the lift starts to sink again. At the end of the night, everyone is in the basement. All drinkers know that place. Here is where there are few words, and most communication is in gestures, expressions, grunts, and moans. And it's not only words that fail you; memory does too. At the same time this is the place where strong bonds are forged between people. If you stay on the tenth floor while all of your friends have descended to the basement, they are suspicious of you—not hostile, but wondering why you don't want to join them there.

The only people who speak to drunks using complete sentences are the police and their wives or girlfriends. For this reason complete sentences are received as subliminal threats from someone in authority. Today, as a non-drinker, I can feel the well of goodwill drain as the night wears on at a bar and the good cheer between drinkers extends less and less to me. Alcohol and drugs make users indecipherable to outsiders. But if you are one of them—and I once was one of them—you speak in a code that fills in the blanks with expressions or gestures. Non-users can understand the words, but the words alone don't mean much to them. If you want to hear people speaking in complete sentences and paragraphs, you go to the Siam Society.

I liked bars when I drank. I liked the people I met in them. I liked taking that trip down to the basement of insensibility that seemed ultra-cool and profound. I liked the drunks, the bar owners and managers, the customers, the punks, the liars, the cheats, the veterans, the men on the run from authorities or ex-wives or their old lives. I talked to them, drank with them, wrote about them.

In the years since I last had a drink, I've gradually eased off hanging out in bars. I've tried to find that old magic in the bar conversation, but there is a barrier that goes up between a drinker and a non-drinker that is difficult to overcome. When you don't drink, someone will always ask, "Why aren't you drinking?" Non-drinkers make drinkers uncomfortable in the way Old People make New People uncomfortable. You worry about someone whose memory is out of alignment with your own.

I can try to mimic the bar patter, but it never works. Even a drunk can detect the dishonesty in a non-drinker acting as if his brain is taking a long whiskey bath. I miss the occasional spontaneous moment of genuine exchange. But my memory of bar drinking days is fading. I pull out those old experiences when I find myself at the terminal, boarding a flight to the land of nostalgia, where the past was much better than the present. That is a Rosy Retrospection flight that it is best to miss because it drops you in a land filled with rose-tinted memories and not much else. What I remember most about my drinking days was that the right bar was a great place to investigate a community or a culture, to take the pulse of the age, and to hear its half-disembodied voices talk about fears, dreams, and beliefs. The right bar was place where people shared memories and made new ones, and in the process found themselves part of a community. The collective memory found in such places is the wool that writers like me gather to knit their stories.

The best time in a bar is before ten in the evening. Drinkers are cranked up. They are halfway down the elevator shaft. The basement is still hours away. In that golden time the liquor gives the drinker confidence to talk about things he's been unwilling to discuss when cold sober. This is the time when you learn the reality of people's lives, the truth of their circumstances, as well as the power of their convictions. Chemicals flush out secrets from our mental hiding places. We remember things, and the next thing we know, we've shared the memory.

Phnom Penh, like Bangkok, has an expat drinking culture. Walk into almost any bar on Street 104 or Street 136 and you'll find foreigners drinking. In the deep future I wonder if alcohol and drugs will be seen as a primitive form of virtual reality. Our distant descendants may view it the way we would look at the use of a fifth-century sundial to co-ordinate the timing of an assembly line, to launch a rocket into space, or to test Einstein's theory of the speed of light. The accuracy of modern timing devices has rendered the sundial crude, primitive, and unreliable. You couldn't base a systematic, global commercial empire on sundial technology. But there is a risk in ignoring the past and looking down at people who inhabited the sundial time as information-challenged simpletons with nothing important to teach us. To make acquaintance with state-of-the-art technology a kind of intelligence test is a mistake. In fact our memories may be more compromised than those of thinkers from the fifth century.

Alcohol remains the same in 2017 as it was in the fifth century, creating the same effect. Our memories are altered by the chemical reaction that drinking causes inside our wet brains as they float inside our small, vulnerable skulls. We drink and do drugs because it's the only way we can recode our memory database. For the finer points of memory, like a sundial used to measure small increments of time, these chemicals are useless but when viewed in the big landscape of distinguishing light from dark, they work very well.

Virtual reality will be a much deeper experience than alcohol, however, and the associated memory ordering, gathering, storage, and use will result in very different ideas about memory. Those who will come after us will join vast networks of thought, experiences, recollections, histories, statistical forecasts, and predictive analysis. That virtual reality won't be experienced; it will rewrite our code at the unconscious level. It will be the ghostwriter of our memories.

That takes me back to my Beverly Hills Polo Club shirt problem. Why was it a problem? It might be better to call it a delusion. I used selective perception and memory processing to reach my false belief that the shirt had belonged to someone who rode polo ponies at an actual polo club. Once I believed it to be true, I did everything I could to confirm that belief. Everything I had learned about the world, what I'd seen, heard, or read, told me that I held before me the physical trace of a genuine polo rider who had checked into my no-star hotel suite some weeks or years before wearing this high-class club's shirt. My memory effortlessly translated the words found on a shirt, and who was I to question the bent of my own mind? That was the problem. I went to automatic pilot without questioning the easy, non-thinking conclusion. I assumed the shirt belonged to a real polo club. My understanding of the clues on the shirt was dead wrong. I'd been as wildly off the mark as if I'd been looking at the moon through the wrong end of a sixteenth-century telescope, or reading the speed of light from a sundial and making predictions about the orbits of planets. Perhaps I had to face it—I'd been living in Asia too long. In the most charitable reading of the incident, my processing proved itself to be nothing special and likely mirrored the way most people perceive and process the little mysteries of life.

I thought my little mystery had the makings of a great story—"Rich Beverly Hills polo player loses shirt in rundown hotel in the heart of Phnom Penh's red light district." How many times had my desire to find a narrative thread affected my perception? Many times. It's a hazard of story-telling for a living: telling a good story means closing down your analytical reasoning, testing, probing, counterarguments, and skepticism. I trained as a lawyer and trained lawyers as a law professor. Apparently at some point I left that part of my memory on the library shelf. Besides, I wanted my polo shirt story to be true. It's difficult when anything you believe to be true turns out, with further examination, to be false. No one likes to admit they've been wrong. That makes memory updates difficult to process as the new information is ignored. I thought I had learned to be aware and avoid this bias. Like a recurring case of asthma, the biases return because avoiding them is not in your control. What I learned instead is that you can be intellectually aware of multiple possibilities for the meaning of an object but still emotionally need that object to stand for only one.

I wanted an illusion of reality to be the real McCoy. The greater illusion is how we think about our memories. It is difficult to wrap our minds around the idea that *all* of our memories are *physical processes* manufactured and stored in the brain. Your memory of your parents, for instance, has a physical presence in your brain. Memories aren't free-floating messages from an ethereal world we visit when we remember someone or something. That's why brain injuries or disease can destroy memories; the physical location can no longer produce the "memory" product.

The physical aspect of memory encoding, storage, and retrieval also suggests how propaganda manipulates the physical processes of memory to create its collective worldview. That worldview is a physical presence, and once in place, self-censorship and self-monitoring are natural and automatic outcomes as we protect our memory system from attack. Mind control has always been the holy grail of power-hungry religions and ideologies. Breaking free of the physical memory jail is a lifelong struggle. As a writer you find yourself either challenging memories or confirming them. George Orwell's literary work often touches upon collective memory and the power of the state, as when he wrote, "The most effective way to destroy people is to deny and obliterate their own understanding of their history."

THIRTEEN

Phnom Penh for the past twenty-five years has been a portal where I've docked, filled up my memory chips, and slipped away. I wrote *Zero Hour in Phnom Penh* in 1993. It was published in 1994, and since then it has been reprinted, translated, and even awarded literary prizes. A small world of readers and critics embraced the novel. In reality it was a blip on the international crime fiction screen, one of those books that if you blinked would have ripped past you without a ripple in the fabric of time. That is the fate of most books. Part of our collective memory of the past is scattered in millions of such books. They are everywhere one moment, and the next moment the vast sea of information has swallowed them up like a whale feeding on plankton.

Many years passed before I wrote about Cambodia again. I had an idea of expanding my vision of the place and time through the voices of many authors, and that gave birth to the anthology *Phnom Penh Noir* (2012). My novella titled "Reunion" appeared in it. It was a story about memory—that of a journalist and that of a former child soldier he'd helped rescue from a refugee camp many years in the past. The boy was delivered to a new life in the United States, but unbeknownst to the journalist, he has since fallen into criminal gang life and then grown into manhood in an

American prison. Having been deported to Cambodia upon his release, he looks up the journalist whose intervention changed his life. The present time in which they are reunited arrives with a lot of luggage from the past, and as the misconceptions, lies, and excuses of the refugee camp days and the Khmer Rouge period are unpacked, the two men find a new way to live in the present.

Like most writers I've been a messenger of memory. It can be delivered in fiction or in non-fiction. Sometimes there can be a bridge between the two, constructed over an abyss of terror and suffering. I've tried that form, too.

At the heart of "Reunion" is a story of memory and forgetting that links it to *Zero Hour in Phnom Penh*. Both are fictional accounts mixed with real events and real people. The anchor of reality is too strong for a writer to cut and sail forth solely on the winds of imagination. Writers of fiction who claim they've invented their characters and stories purely from their imagination, and that none of their work bears any relation to actual events, are either liars or charlatans. Let's be charitable. Such writers may convince themselves that they're only using the raw material to fashion something quite apart from the actual events. But that is an illusion. Writers are memory consolidators of their time, and to play that role well, we are part of a memory chain. We need to write stories of our time that are worth remembering. The aspiration is to pass those stories to the next generation who log them into their memory.

I had the chance in 2011 as an accredited journalist to cover the opening of the Khmer War Crime Tribunal on the outskirts of Phnom Penh. It had been eighteen years since UNTAC soldiers had patrolled the streets. I'd gone on assignment by the *Phnom Penh Post* thanks to arrangements made by an Australian friend, David Armstrong, with the blessing of the *Post*'s management. During my legal career, I had written about social justice issues, but whether qualified or not, this event was one I would not have missed.

My report of the opening day of the trial was the longest report ever printed in the *Phnom Penh Post*. I opened the long essay with this description:

> At 9:00 a.m., Monday, 21 November 2011, the beige curtains were slowly peeled back before an audience of roughly 600 people. The moment was like something out of *The Wizard of Oz*: the expectation of what lies behind the levers of power inevitably results in disappointment.
>
> Three men in their 80s sat on the right side of the chambers. Each of the trio was charged with crimes against humanity, genocide and violations of the Geneva Conventions. Along with Pol Pot, these men had been top Khmer Rouge policymakers. As the political architects of death that defined the Khmer Rouge, they were on trial before a court of law.
>
> Seated with the accused, their lawyers, dressed in black gowns, listened to the charges against their clients. Uniformed security personnel kept the accused under a watchful eye. At 9:05 a.m., everyone on both sides of the glass enclosure stood as seven robed judges filed in and took their places on the bench.
>
> Four of the judges were Cambodian; the remaining three were from New Zealand, Austria and France. As the court was called to order, everyone in the court and gallery took their seats. Case 002 had commenced. History was being made. As a law professor and lawyer,

I have experienced the ritual of courtrooms in Canada, the United States, England, Malaysia and Thailand, with the opposing counsel at their tables, the judges on the bench and the accused in the dock.

Courtrooms are a form of ancient theatre, where the players have defined roles and the procedures are formal and the decor somber. Objective, fair, rational decision making is the premise for the deliberation. Justice is the goal. Everyone is assigned a role to play. The Extraordinary Chambers in the Courts of Cambodia (ECCC) was specifically built for the trial of the men and women who occupied leadership positions during the Khmer Rouge reign of terror.

The courtroom physically separated its participants and the audience with a large wall of glass. Inside the fishbowl were the officials, judges, lawyers and security personnel. Courts are public storytelling venues. The prosecution carries the burden of telling the story to establish guilt. On this Monday, the prosecution laid out its case.

On the Tuesday, the accused made opening arguments in their own defense. They denied their responsibility for the crimes for which they were accused. As the trial proceeds, they will call witnesses and enter evidence to establish a counter narrative, such as that they acted to repel foreign invaders and to safeguard Cambodia.

Over the months and years to follow, the prosecution will introduce evidence supporting the charges. Then, the accused will be given an opportunity to present his or her side of the story. They continue to refuse to accept that they did anything wrong. This should come as no surprise, as it remains consistent with the mindset that formulated the policies for the killing fields.

I hadn't come here to witness a "normal" murder trial. Not even the trial of the worst serial killer approached the body count attributed to the policies of these three men. Their crimes were an order of magnitude beyond anyone's experience of homicide cases.

The systematic killing saw the scaling of murder to an industrial level. Men, women and children by the truckload were murdered day after day, for years, with no break between the killings. I observed the accused over the course of the proceedings as the Cambodian co-prosecutor read her opening statement.

The audience present for the opening statement was filled with ordinary Cambodians. They had come to witness the Khmer Rouge leadership, whose policies had visited death upon nearly every Cambodian family.

Ordinary Cambodians, students, relatives of victims and survivors all sat side by side in the audience to gaze upon the faces of the men who had unleashed the nightmare. The proceedings were also broadcast throughout Cambodia.

People in the remote countryside and in the cities and towns could watch on television or listen on the radio. The entire population of Cambodia finally had their chance after 32 years to hear details of the charges laid against the three accused.

This was far more than a legal proceeding; it was a place where those who had caused the killing fields would be judged. Not many ever thought that day would come. Or, if it did, that they would witness the proceedings. Yet, there they were, watching, remembering, coming to terms with the past, and searching the faces of those on the other side of the glass for answers.

The title of the essay was *Killing fields justice: A witness to history being made.* When I read that essay now I realize the importance of memory and how the physical process underlying memory is extremely difficult to change. The Old People had their memories of the Khmer Rouge locked up in their brains; the trial wasn't going to be a key to unlock their mental doors and replace the old memories with new ones. Our memories don't work like that. The trial would be a success if its local and international observers could be satisfied that the "facts" submitted in evidence constituted a memorial for the New People who had suffered the most casualties under the Khmer Rouge.

When I look back on covering that opening day of the trial, I recognize the first seeds of this memory project of subsequent years. What I was witnessing was confirming George Orwell's observation that the most thorough means of destroying a people is through the destruction of its history. The task of such tribunals is never simple. While one side will argue that the proceedings will clarify and illuminate history, the other side will plead that they exist for the purpose of denial and obliteration.

The Cambodian war crimes trial followed a long negotiation over the legal process and the question of who would be hauled before the court. The court was sold to its international backers as an exercise in collectively remembering the Khmer Rouge genocide, understanding it, assigning responsibility for it, and setting the historical record straight. Eventually the effort would fall short of that ideal. What we remember and what we forget have political consequences, in this case consequences for how the memory of this period would be preserved. Not everyone wants the same things to be retained in collective memory. Everyone has a list of events and personalities they wish others to forget. In this case the mandate of the court, the selection of the judges, the choice of whom to prosecute, the nature of the charges, and the involvement of the public (even the location of where to build the courthouse complex) were politically driven. The developed world financed this historical memory exercise.

On the first day of the proceedings—it was like the opening night of a play or a film—I ran into a lot of old friends such as Seth Mydans, correspondent for the *New York Times*, and James Pringle (a legend in journalism, who had been Beijing Bureau Chief for *Newsweek*) and his Cambodian-born wife, Milly. Outside the courtroom we talked with Cambodian students who had come to witness the proceedings. Milly asked several students in Khmer what they knew about the Khmer Rouge and the killing fields. They smiled and shrugged; they knew almost nothing about what had happened. Their parents and relatives hadn't discussed the genocide. It wasn't a subject taught in school. It wasn't written about in material that young people would read. The memory of the Khmer Rouge had not lodged itself in the minds of the young generation of Cambodians. When in 1993 I'd asked Cambodians this question, everyone had remembered a relative, a neighbor, a teacher, or a friend who'd been killed or died of starvation or disease. What had happened to those memories? The answer is that in the succeeding eighteen years, a new generation of young people had been born. It was as if the brains of most of them returned a blank screen when asked about the crimes of Pol Pot and his leadership.

Memory is like a traveling salesman; it always has something to sell you. But there are gaps in memory's inventory. It sells what is most profitable and easy to sell. Sadly, there is no profit in remembering genocide or identifying the killers beyond a small handful who take the blame for the thousands who participated in the slaughter. The full weight of our global consumer society fits well with the aspirations of tyrants; the two forces work together to place boundaries on our collective memories. The tribunal was erected to work inside a dictatorship and financed by global capitalist-controlled governments in the West. The court had all the trappings of a feel-good exercise. It was a judicial Disneyland, with old men in the dock as evil villains. None of the defendants in the dock had personally killed anyone. There was blood on the hands of many people in Cambodia from that time, but they weren't in the dock; they weren't even in the audience. The defendants played the role of people to hate, the role of those responsible for ordering terrible things, and as in a Greek drama, we sat with the chorus listening to the lawyers make speeches.

Show trials historically are short and sweet, often a formality preceding a bullet in the back of the head for the accused. The Cambodian war crimes trial dragged on until the media attention of that first day, which focused the world on remembering the Khmer Rouge's killing fields, ran out of steam. The attention of the international community shifted. Memories of those who experienced this period faded. In 2017 on the river cruise I asked some young Cambodians about the war crimes tribunal. They hadn't heard of it. It was a beautiful evening on the Tonle Sap River and the sun was setting in one of those postcard perfect splashes of color. The Khmer Rouge death squads weren't part of the day.

Phnom Penh sunset from Toule Sap 2017

Living in the moment has a downside. What we remember isn't found in the moment; it comes from what our brains have encoded from the past. As the sun set and we drifted on the boat, our minds drifted too, scattering and extinguishing our thoughts like the fading light.

The first day of the war crimes tribunal trial, I thought like other journalists that there was a chance to consolidate memories of the Khmer Rouge period. But the scope of the investigation into what happened and who participated in the killing fields was narrowed, reduced to a token. A broad mandate to examine all war crimes was a hard sell to the strongman of the Cambodian government, who was himself an ex-Khmer Rouge cadre. Hun Sen, prime minister of Cambodia from 1985 to today, warned more than once that venturing too deeply into history would start a new civil war. The forces of Old People and New People hadn't reconciled. Maybe they never could. By February 2017 the tribunal was still deciding whether a case could proceed against a Khmer Rouge official. It dismissed the case against Im Chaem, a former Khmer Rouge district commander who ran one of the forced labor camps. The court decided she hadn't played a senior enough role to be held accountable.

Cambodia has been a high-stakes memory game. The Old People have won the pot sometimes, and the New People have also had their victories. The process has been more about maintaining the peace between the two factions than finding the historical facts and identifying who was involved in carrying out the genocide. The tribunal made a calculated political decision in Im Chaem's case, one that would have not surprised Orwell, who wrote, "Political language is designed to make lies sound truthful and murder respectable, and to give an appearance of solidity to pure wind."

We look to memory for the truth of the past. We are disappointed when we discover people have different memories from ours, and contrary truths. The search for a one-size-fits-all truth worth preserving is mainly the work of public relations. Survivorship bias leads us to focus on people who walked away from the genocide and overlook those buried in the ground. The dead aren't visible. They don't have desires, needs, or demands. They are no longer contributing to the memory game. It's their silence that excludes them from the day-to-day life of the survivors. The survivors of the Cambodian genocide and their children and grandchildren were more concerned about food, disease, schools, and housing than history; those preoccupations bolted them securely to the floor of the present. The shantytown communities along the river weren't holding discussion groups to discuss the Khmer Rouge experiences, the murders, and the tribunal. They were far more likely to be talking about the price of rice and how to raise the money to buy granny some medicine.

FOURTEEN

What we don't experience on a personal level leaves a void in our episodic memory. But the absence of experience is no deterrent to our forming strong beliefs about what happened or who did what to whom. Like beachcombers we pick up information as we go along, and some of that information we remember. We source these memories from second-hand accounts, gossip, rumors, propaganda, the reports of slanted news media, comments on timelines, and books. We absorb a steady daily intake of large amounts of information. Each piece of it bids for our attention and for an upload into our semantic memory.

Our library systems face a similar information overload problem every year: which books to add to the shelves and which to remove from them. Like libraries our brains have a management system that classifies and integrates memories into our collection. Even if you are blessed with an exceptional memory, you've thrown away much more of the information you've processed over a lifetime than you've retained. Most of us can't even remember everything that we experienced or read or were told earlier today. There's a limited amount of shelf space in our memory. On the societal level, as with the history of the war crimes tribunal in Cambodia and similar reckonings throughout history, usually it's the politicians and the bureaucrats, uniformed and armed, who act as librarians with centurion paranoia, deciding what information is selected and what is ignored, and whose account of the past will continue to be available and whose will be banned. Be aware of the architects who design the model of your world.

Intellectually we can understand the library metaphor, but emotionally our memory "feels" complete, permanent, and unlimited in capacity. Where in the brain is the mechanism where our subjective view is generated? We fight over memories, but we rarely ask how memories are physically located in our brains. No one can point a finger and say, "Look here. That's the place." The inner workings of the human brain and the chemical and electrical processes involved remain, as far as memory is concerned, largely a mystery. From the neuroscience research available today we know bits and pieces about the structure and function of the brain's management system and the co-ordination of the brain's parts, but there is much more that we don't know.

Part of what scientists believe now about modular brain network organization may still prove to be wrong or woefully incomplete. We are in the early days of brain exploration. The drive to understand the brain's organization aligns with our technological society's interest in developing artificial intelligence as a rival organization with the goal to expand information retention. What you remember within your own brain is a co-operative effort inside that network organization, one that you perceive without any of the very real seams, borders, or cracks that lie between the various assembled parts of the network. That smooth, subjective perception emerges as a story we tell to ourselves and to others. Our very brain organization disposes us all to be natural-born story-tellers.

The current state of neuroscience recalls a parallel stage that early mapmakers went through. Our oldest surviving maps were made by Christian cartographers who carefully pinpointed the Garden of Eden and other landmarks and features of the Bible. Those worlds they mapped were more dreamy theme parks of belief than physical places. For example, European maps in the Middle Ages placed Jerusalem at the center of the earth. That was the nature of medieval faith. Similarly, in our own time, consciousness, subjectivity, qualia, and memory are largely unknown, fabled lands, and like the location of the Garden of Eden, the subject of conjecture. Some equivalent of today's GPS precision lies in the future of humanity's exploration of its own brain function and brain organization.

The relationship of memory and sleep is a good example of an aspect of brain function that we understand imperfectly if at all. All animals sleep. Why has evolution produced animals that require sleep? It is a legitimate question. An answer starts with understanding that the human brain contains about 100 billion neurons. Those neurons are wired to communicate through electromagnetic signals traveling through a system of synapses linking them in a network so they can work together. Those 100 billion neurons are linked by 100 trillion synapses.

When I remember a sunset on the Tonle Sap or the faces of the old men on trial at the war crime tribunal, my synaptic system delivers these images through a strong physical link among many neurons working together. The stronger the associated synapses, it has been argued, the more accessible and fixed is the memory in the neurons docked to those synapses. If all our synapses were pushed to maximum strength, we would have no room for any further memories. Forgetting gets a bad rap. Without forgetting, the system would quickly overload and bar new memories from entering. Epilepsy is a condition caused by overloaded, stretched-out synapses, and at a tipping point, the system crashes and we witness a seizure. A healthy brain regulates the synaptic system by scaling down the strength of these neuron connections.

During sleep these synapses shrink and the brain loses its ability to access most memories. Only the strong, emotionally charged memories survive the cleansing of the memory house during sleep. Without that clearing, that descaling, we'd lack the ability to lay down new memories or access existing ones—to master a new language, for instance, or to recall the faces and names of our family, friends, and neighbors, or to recognize the danger of a mad dog. There is a Darwinian element to sleep and memory. Memory is mostly about survival; everything else is a bonus. Mostly what you forget, you don't need in order to survive. There are other memories, so terrible and frightening, that we repress them as best we can. But we aren't in full control of what our brain remembers and forgets. It is a system we are forced to work with, but it isn't a perfect system that guarantees to advance our optimal decision-making. It is just good enough. Ed Yong analyzed current research in the science of sleep in his *Atlantic* article titled *The Brain's Connections Shrink During Sleep* (2017).

Watch a movie or read a book. Then go for two days without sleep. Take an examination on what you saw or read. Your brain will have lost its opportunity to rescale its synapses. Chances are you won't be able to access what should have been your memories of the movie or the book to answer the examination questions. All of the information that entered your brain then and since has prevented your neurons from sorting through the images and words and consolidating them into usable memory. The information may be there, somewhere in the neurons, but you have no way to access it. We call that forgetting. We sleep to remember, and the cost of remembering is forgetting information that isn't connected to some emotional jolt strong enough to pump up the synapses, allowing it to survive the rescaling that occurs during sleep.

When your head hits the pillow tonight, say good night to the 100 trillion synapses that your brain will be downscaling, cleaning up the scraps of information about your day, the smudges of color, sound, smell, taste, and touch you encountered, the faces on the train home from work, the name of a street you were on, who directed the movie you saw, and a thousand other details that passed through your sensory perception. In the morning that information will be gone. It is the start of a new day with more new information, soon to be followed by another night of cleansing. Sisyphus wasn't rolling a boulder up the side of a mountain. He was rolling a massive bundle of information up a mental incline every day, only to have it roll back down every night.

FIFTEEN

Quay, Toule Sap, Phnom Penh 2017

The sharing of values, ideas, and information combine to create a collective consciousness. These memories form a solid sense of solidarity with others. Your store of common memories and knowledge is your group membership identification badge. Our hive minds share these memories through a common language, vocabulary, and style of speech. We can test the social membership of others by asking certain questions about language. Fail the test, and you will be surprised if not shocked as the "togetherness" dissolves and you are excluded from the hive.

About twenty years ago the English novelist Timothy Mo, whom I had known for some years and who had become a friend, asked me how I pronounced the word "quay." Why I would remember that conversation while on a river cruise in Phnom Penh is a mystery. Shouldn't it have been washed away after a night of sleep? But there it was—the image of Timothy and me, walking on Beach Road in Pattaya. I thought Timothy's question was an odd thing to ask and perhaps a trick question, a test. The precise pronunciation seemed quite important to him, or at the very least my pronunciation of "quay" had meaning for him.

"Do you say 'kee' or do you say 'kwai'?" he pressed me.

"Kwai," I said.

"Like an American," he said with a hint of disdain in his voice.

Right, I thought, you failed the literacy test. Back to the boat that brought you, and don't come back.

In 2017 I was remembering this minor conversation but with no understanding of why. I'd not talked to Timothy in years. He'd gone underground like J.D. Salinger. Apparently he'd rescaled his memory and my details had been cleansed from his synapses. Watching the sun set over Phnom Penh, it came to me what I should have said all those years ago: "In Thai, 'kwai' translates as water buffalo. Mind you, there is a need to get the tone right. 'Kee' in Thai means shit—not shit exclusive to a water buffalo. It covers all shit from all orifices. To complicate matters, the Thai pronunciation of *quay* means penis. If you have to choose between pronunciation that means water buffalo, shit or penis, does it really matter? The fact is the English say shit (for Q-U-A-Y and North Americans say water buffalo, but objectively how can one be preferred to the other? It's all usage. Or should we disturb the language god (who isn't English or American) for an answer?"

That little speech is embarrassing to share with you now. It diminishes me in my own eyes. What exactly was at stake in that brief exchange that I should carry this memory with me all of those years? There I was in Phnom Penh, composing an elaborate and defensive response to what likely was a minor chance remark. That is one of the dangers of memory: it can reduce you in your own eyes, and then you want to detach yourself from the feelings that were strong enough to keep those synapses strong and enduring, when so much other information was carried out to sea and deep-sixed.

This isn't a bug in human memory; it's a feature. We don't have full agency over what goes and what stays, or fully understand the process of our own brain's operation. We are shut off from knowing how we know, how we remember, and why we forget one conversation yesterday and remember another twenty years before. As information-processing entities that deeply believe in our own individuality, we cling to the idea that our memories belong to us, we earned them, we experienced them, and no one has a dataset stored in their brain quite like mine or yours. In a social setting, it is the collective memories that form collectively conscious communities. We are always being tested. Each examination confirms or denies that our memories and knowledge appropriately fit the collective identity of the group. The different pronunciation of a single word may be sufficient to get you banished.

SIXTEEN

Authors, like ants, pick up the scent trails of those who preceded them. In my case, I've been tracking the literary pheromone trail left by writers such as George Orwell, Graham Green, Timothy Mo, Paul Theroux, and Anthony Burgess. Each of them set memorable books in Southeast Asia or thereabouts. One such trail was left by Somerset Maugham. His *The Moon and Sixpence* relates the story of a British stockbroker who abandons his London life to be a painter in Paris and then Tahiti, a tale based on the life of Paul Gauguin. Since Maugham's novel, writers have kept one eye peeled for the next European painter who abandons job, family, and ordinary life to feverishly paint exotic young women in their native setting. As every generation of ants builds a nest much like those of the previous generations, it is no surprise that a future Gauguin would fall into the hands of a new author/worker ant building a new literary nest. Maugham locked in our collective memory the romantic, talented, half-mad, half-genius artist who painted memories for a new generation to experience.

In recent years two expat artists have entered Cambodia's street life with the tenacity of Gauguin. Chris Coles, an American from Maine, had been a university radical at Brown, protesting the Vietnam War. To evade the draft, he escaped to Africa and led the CIA on a fruitless one-year chase through Idi Amin's Uganda. After the Americans canceled his passport, he convinced the Austrian embassy to give him a refugee passport—allegedly the only American ever to receive such a passport—and he used it to travel to attend film school in London. Coles's thumb in the eye to overreaching authority, his history of being on the run and of working in Hollywood (taking advantage of the Carter amnesty for those who avoided the draft, he returned to the States), prepared him for Southeast Asia's noir landscapes filled with gangsters, pimps, prostitutes, tourists, and neon-lit streets lined with bars. He brought an impressionist eye to the underworld of late-night Bangkok and Phnom Penh.

Coles maintained a studio not far from another painter who had come to Phnom Penh to capture the city's spirit, faces, moods, and ambiance and the toll it took on the lives of the locals who did what they had to do to survive. The paintings of Dutch-born artist Peter Klashorst have a surreal, nightmarish screaming-through-fire feeling. Coles's painting of Klashorst captures this controlled artistic vision that sometimes tips into visual insanity.

Chris Coles portrait of Peter Klaushorst

Chris Coles has painted the portraits of many of the characters who are part of life in Phnom Penh. His noir style is reflected in his painting of me.

Chris Coles portrait of Christopher G. Moore

One might consider both artists mandala builders but of different kinds. Chris Coles's mandala creates a surreal, noir series of gateways from the hells of Phnom Penh; these are the way he symbolizes the people and the city. Coles's dark vision of the human soul, roiled by larger forces, seeks to overcome four false gateways: those of the corrupt, the tainted, the tormented, and the lost. Peter Klashorst's mandala burns the consciousness with cartoonish characters of fantasy who mingle with distorted images of the present. Religious icons, nudes, politicians, sexual perverts, historical figures, and horses gallop through his paintings, crashing through every mandala gateway like a terrorist wishing to scorch the earth with his painted anger and frustration. Coles's artistic travels take him far beyond Phnom Penh to the political world of America and the night world of

Bangkok. Klashorst's tortured soul burns with passion and draws him to Phnom Penh where he spends most of his time. He is rooted in the city and its culture. He's known nothing in life but painting. He's never had another avocation or job. He paints to live and lives to paint. Like Gauguin, his mandala spins with the dark-energy forces that explode from within.

The possibility of discovering a contemporary Paul Gauguin occurred to me when I had the chance to meet Klashorst, who had studios in Phnom Penh and Bangkok. Like Gauguin, Peter had a life that had been messy, filled with betrayals, court cases, children left behind, and controversy.

In 2017 I'd come to Phnom Penh to check in on him. He had AIDS, and his health had taken a turn for the worse, so he was back taking his medicine. Two years earlier, I'd produced a video titled "The Impatient Artist," shot at Peter's Bangkok studio. The camera crew taped as Peter painted my portrait and we discussed art, life, and creativity. Peter's Bangkok studio could have passed for a CIA black site, where the suspect, in this case me, was seated on a tiled floor in a jacket and scarf, with no air-conditioning and no fan. It was the little-known cousin to waterboarding: the video sweat-out ceremony. There my own recording device, my memory, was laying down the claustrophobic feeling of trying to maintain composure while every biological alarm rang. Now when I look at the finished painting, my memory returns to the black-and-white photographs displayed at Tuol Sleng, the genocide museum on the site of the former S-21 prison. The Khmer Rouge had photographed every prisoner who'd passed through the former schoolhouse on the way to execution, leaving behind a difficult-to-match record of what a face expresses on its way to a communal grave.

My example of how a memory can attach itself to other memories betrays the potential shallowness and distortion of such connections. No matter how uncomfortable I'd been in Peter's studio, I'd gone there voluntarily. Moreover, it was I who had arranged the time and place along with the presence of the film crew. I had been in control. I had the freedom to leave at any time. What I was forced to endure for a few hours was self-inflicted.

Peter Klaushorst portrait of author 2016

Peter lived an austere life in a walk-up garret on Street 136. Life seen from a cockroach- and rat-infested garret looks different from life observed from a river cruise. I climbed up the narrow, dark concrete stairs reminiscent of ones found in ancient castles—though it would have been difficult to swing a sword on that staircase. At the top of the long flight was a locked metal door like the kind I remember from T-3 Prison. He appeared barefoot and wearing a baggy pair of boxer shorts. No shirt. He looked thinner than I remembered. We went out to the balcony area, where he had been painting. A young Khmer woman was hanging up laundry. Peter always had a young Khmer somewhere on the premises. They spent most of the time on their cellphones (financed by Peter), talking to their mothers, boyfriends, or customers. None of those conversations bothered Peter. He thought it natural they'd have customers and another boyfriend or two.

He nodded at the young woman hanging up one of his shirts on a clothesline. "I don't know why she's doing that. She's never done my laundry before. But she wants money for Chinese New Year. I have to give it to her. I'm broke but I still have to pay her."

The clothesline sagged across the balcony, obscuring the view of Street 136. Not long after I settled into my chair, we heard shouting and cursing from the street below. A man's voice rang the bell of anger. People emerged from bars and shops in the street to watch the public theatre performance with its age-old script featuring a domestic quarrel. Peter and I went to the balcony and watched as a woman in a flower-patterned dress and sandals quickly walked down the street, chased by a shouting old man ten meters behind her. He had a bum leg and was having trouble catching up. Stopping, she turned, waved her fist, and told him to fuck off. But there was a lack of conviction in her voice. He was slow but determined, and the harassed woman could see that he was closing the distance between them. She turned and broke into a half-run. Their exchange was in Khmer, but reading their body language and facial expressions, I had no doubt that the woman expected to be beaten if she let the man catch her.

"She runs things on the street. Beggars, whores, and underground lottery numbers. Everyone hates her."

"Is that her husband?" I asked, watching her pick up the hem of her dress as she increased her stride.

She wasn't moving all that fast. The exertion showed on her face as she passed under the balcony.

"It's just some local she's pissed off. Maybe he'll kill her. It happens," said Peter in matter-of-fact Dutch-accented English. "No one would miss her. Someone would take her place in a few hours, and after a week no one would remember her name."

"Why would he kill her?"

"In Phnom Penh, it's no good to ask such a question."

Peter had known Andy Warhol and Robert Mapplethorpe when he'd lived in New York City in the early 1980s. I'd lived downtown in Soho around the same time. There was a lot of crime there back then: murders, robberies, stabbings. You wouldn't find that there today. It only exists in the memories of people who experienced it. But Peter and I never met in New York. In my years in Southeast Asia I'd encountered various ex-New Yorkers who'd lived through those times (John Fengler, for example), and our memories of the city cemented a personal bond, as it did between Peter and me. These people and I had been through something together—not quite a war, but high crime areas and war zones merge at some juncture. We could share our memories of the music, the drugs, the comedy clubs, the small theatre companies performing in garages, the porno videos sold off dirty blankets by young men constantly looking out for the cops, and the shell games of con artists cheating people on Canal Street. This often-revisited connection through New York in that period made it easy to fall into Carl Jung's idea of synchronicity. If you were a Jungian, you might read our convergence in Phnom Penh as a meaningful coincidence, a paranormal connection that had nothing to do with causation. This version of synchronicity was a falling together in time of people linked to a common memory of a place and time that had shaped the people they had become. We recognized something of ourselves, bits of memory that we shared, in one another.

The floors and walls of Peter's studio were covered with paintings with political, sexual, and religious images—sometimes all three in the same work, such as Trump in a Nazi uniform with a broken cross and a young woman with her legs spread, showing her pinkish labia. Large breasts, rounded hips, and full lips appeared under McDonald's signs. Those paintings had got him into trouble. He'd gone to prison in Africa for painting local nubile women in the nude. The Dutch media vilified him. He was their enfant terrible, their bad boy. Facebook periodically shut him down for violating their rules on showing images of naked people. Facebook censorship robots had sent him notices referring to his latest posting of a nude woman sucking the penis of a famous politician. Facebook algorithms, like Judge Dredd, made a nanosecond's verdict—Peter's artistic defacing of a politician wasn't an exercise of free political speech but pornography, for which he was banned. Obscenity is a class of image we don't want people to remember, so it is shut down and the pornographers banished and chased into the hills.

Peter was suffering through one of those periods when his revenues had dwindled to zero, and yet there was always another girl who wanted him to buy her an iPhone. Facebook's censorship was causing havoc in the local economy around Street 136, upsetting the balance.

"They leave other people's art alone," Peter said, during one of our discussions about Facebook. "But they don't like me."

"Why do you think that?" I asked him.

"I painted Mark Zuckerberg fucking a pig."

"I doubt he cares," I said. "He'd think you were trying to get attention. That you'd watched *Black Mirror* too many times."

"That's the problem. No one fucking cares. Nothing shocks people."

Sometimes Peter could be profound. Unlike most profound people who got distracted by their eloquence, Peter doggedly went back to his original grievance with the Facebook censors.

He picked up a brush from a can on the floor and tipped it in a one-liter red pail. "If it's not him, it's one of those cowards in Holland who want everyone to think I paint porn. I paint the consumer society. It's capitalism that consumes these young women, not me. They are the true pornographers and they make a fortune. No one can touch them. The people in Holland hate me because of those people. Some old bitch emailed Facebook asking them to look at my paintings and then ask why they *should have* to look at them. It's just stupid. No one is forcing anyone to look at my paintings or god forbid, buy one. Why don't they fuck off?"

Now Peter had drifted into philosophy. Why didn't most people leave others alone?

With Facebook off limits as a place to sell his paintings, Peter continued to paint even though he sold nothing and couldn't pay his bills. Cambodia was many things, but one thing it wasn't was a haven for wealthy patrons of the arts who appreciated what Peter was doing. He had no choice but to sell his paintings through the Internet. Peter had a deep talent for inciting strong emotions in people. In this reaction of others I found a toxic mixture of hatred and anger. His paintings offended their fundamentalist sensibilities and questioned the purity and absolute sanctity they saw as underlying their values. The positions on both sides of the memory divide hardened: the Old People hated Peter, and the New People hated him too. He'd managed to do what few politicians had ever accomplished in Cambodia, Europe, or America: to synchronize the two groups' ancient bicameral hallucinations. Peter hammered, challenged, satirized, and poked Voltaire's walking stick in the eye of authority figures. His obsession with women as disposable, commercial objects to be exchanged, sold, or traded as the ultimate marketable good in consumer society hit these people hard.

I had mixed feelings about some of his paintings. Sometimes they seemed like one Big Mac away from visual purging. But art we value today wasn't always valued when it was first displayed. No one can say which contemporary art will transmit the meta-consciousness that will cleave to the library of our collective memory. Not even the artist knows how this happens. What artist or author hits the target every time? My friend Max, the lawyer, missed the dartboard more than once. All of this is not to detract from the overall effect of Peter's work—he paints to express dissent from and rage at the hypocrisy of the religious and the capitalists who co-operate in opening a global shopping mall where memory has become a mass-produced database with prices attached to everything. We live in an age when artists like Peter make people uncomfortable with their challenges to our political, social, and economic gods.

Peter violated the unwritten code that compels modern commentators to stay within accepted moral bounds of how we experience the world. Anyone who streaks naked across the pitch during half-time isn't deemed to be in the business of political commentary. Such a person was someone to be shut down or he would poison the episodic memory well. That kind of revolt might spread. It should come as no surprise when someone emails Mark Zuckerberg to protest the code violator—"Get this asshole off Facebook. I am a foot soldier in a huge army of believers and Facebook users. We demand you exile this pornographer. Side with us and you prosper; side with Peter Klashorst and we will turn against you."

Memory Manifesto

What happened to Peter dramatizes the modern cultural crisis today in Europe and America—the high church of the pre-Enlightenment is clawing back its position, and artists can no longer use the magic cloak of Voltaire for immunity. There was newfound comfort in the old maps that showed the way among memories. There are millions of people who are still guided by those medieval maps upon which all the destinations of their belief are represented. When artists expose the myth in the mental mapping, they open the dragon's cage and monsters charge into the world. Facebook runs a successful business in the defense of which, when push comes to shove, they will side with the ancient, narrow mind over the mind calling for flexibility and creativity. Money follows the old memory channels. At least for now. Following a future memory big bang all bets are off as to the role money will play once cognitive scarcity is removed from the equation.

SEVENTEEN

I remember seeing Bill Clinton on television during the 2016 presidential campaigns. The image didn't fit my memory. When you live abroad, celebrities, politicians, and public figures can drop off your radar screen for years. Bill, his hair pure white, his face emaciated like he'd just finished the Bataan Death March, his posture slightly stooped, had become an old man. He could have been typecast as the old guy leaning forward from his chair on the front porch, shaking a fist at neighborhood kids, and shouting, "Get off the grass!"

But my memory of Bill Clinton is tied with Cambodia in 1998. He was president then and in major political trouble over lying about a young woman. That was the year Bill Clinton was impeached. On 19 December 1998 I watched the vote in House of Representatives from my room at Phnom Penh's Intercontinental Hotel. Of all the memories I have of Cambodia over the years, why do the memories of Bill Clinton and one night in Phnom Penh back then remain "sticky" in my brain, sticky enough for his appearance on TV to bring that memory back into consciousness? Why hadn't that memory disappeared into oblivion like the vast number of memories that never stick? And how in a little less than two decades had the idea of the lie Bill told become so out of date in a time of "fake news" and "alternative facts"? In 1998 there had been a consensus that the divide between truth and lies was discernible. If you buried your memory of the truth, others would find a way to dig it out. In the new political memory garden all the weeds were seeded by your opponents' lies and all the flowers grown from your own nursery of truth.

We subjectively feel our memories to be true. Perhaps in Bill's mind, when he said that he "did not have sexual relations [intercourse] with that [particular] woman," he believed, rationally, technically, that in a lawyer's courtroom of a world he was telling the truth. Most of us don't live in that world.

In any case, the moment of Bill Clinton's impeachment by the House in 1998 continues to fire the neurons brightly in the places where my brain has preserved it assiduously. But why does this historical American moment "feel" to me like a Cambodian event? As with my retention of Timothy Mo's offhand question to me about the pronunciation of "quay," the answer may lie in the way the brain works.

When we are awake, we are on the receiving end of an unending flow of information from our environment. That information enters into the synaptic system as basic units that are assembled by the brain according to meaning, purpose, and associated pleasure or threat. We may react to a smell or sound but retain no long-term memory of the event. Your social media timeline is processed in the same way. There is pressure on the synapses as they reach capacity limits. The system can only store so much memory. It's like a river where the volume of water threatens to overflow the banks and flood the countryside.

As I've mentioned above, sleep drains that river. Our synaptic system shrinks by around eighteen percent after a night's sleep. Sleep, it seems, drains the mental swamp. This drainage system is a by-product of what evolved as a brain maintenance system. We are born with a built-in factory setting that determines the carrying load of our synaptic system. Because of an evolutionary hack, the system uses sleep to create space for the fresh flow of new memories. Eighteen percent doesn't seem like much new working space, but it is all we have after each night of sleep.

The House of course did end up impeaching Clinton. Five weeks later the Senate acquitted him of perjury and abuse of power charges. His acquittal was on 12 February 1999. I wasn't in Cambodia on that day. I have absolutely no memory of what I was doing on 12 February 1999. I must have been doing something, experiencing life somehow. I know I was writing a book titled *Chairs* around that time. Why do I vividly remember the impeachment roll call and yet have no recollection of witnessing the equally important moment of the acquittal?

A plausible explanation is that with memory storage limited, the information of many of our days is never encoded into long-term memory. That inner brain librarian system is highly selective about what it retains on the one hand and which old and seldom accessed memories it culls on the other. Memories are like muscle mass—use it or lose it. In the case of memory, what seems lost may not be entirely so but rather substantially degraded in reliability and accuracy. Intellectually that is understandable but it doesn't explain why I remember 19 December 1998 in considerable detail but have no recollection of 12 February 1999. Both dates represent important political milestones. You would think the two would have been logged into my memory with equal force, but that wasn't the case. Science does offer an explanation.

It turns out that unusual circumstances, strong emotions, and the strangeness of competing sensory perceptions make the perfect storm for remembering an incident or event.

What do you remember about your sex life? Many memories are like those floaters that cross your path of vision; they pop in and out of reality like virtual particles in a vacuum. But in some cases, powerful flashes or jolts to one or more of the senses deliver an experience that embeds it in your memory. Think for a moment about a memory you have about sex. Unless you are celibate, that sentence will send your brain automatically to a memory file. Sensory aspects of the experience return in an instant. I can share one such moment in Cambodia. I had sex on 19 December 1998. If I had sex on Friday, 12 February 1999, I don't remember it.

When writers put an Orwellian spotlight on the powerful in the name of truth telling, they also needs the courage to turn that light on themselves and let others judge them, revile them, hate them, and scorn them. That is a prelude to my sex story in Cambodia on 19 December 1998, the day the House impeached Bill Clinton. On 25 and 26 November 1996, Bill Clinton visited Bangkok timeon a state visit to Thailand. One of my readers, a US air force pilot stationed in Japan, was in Bangkok and he'd been invited to meet Bill Clinton at an American embassy reception here. The Calvino fan delivered a signed copy of *The Big Weird* to Bill Clinton. A couple of months later, I received a letter via the American embassy on White House stationery, signed by Bill Clinton, thanking me for *The Big Weird*. I suspect Bill's staff sent out thousands of such signed letters. No doubt he understood this was a cheap price to gain lifelong loyalty from a stadium of nobodies. What politician could pass up that kind of opportunity? Bill also had a history of rarely passing up the chance for a quickie. Judge not, less you be judged is a good rule of thumb, except in public office, where that rule is suspended. Like many successful men, Clinton appeared to be a complex amalgam of intellectual genius and testosterone moron.

Bill's clandestine relationship with Monica was one of his more moronic moments. A sitting president had lied about oral sex. He ignored the "oral" part of it and lied about the sex part. In strict legal terms, it was the lie rather than the actual blowjobs that got him in legal trouble. What most people remember is Bill, the miscreant, muttering his double-talk denial. That ill-fated statement may not go on his tombstone but it will likely appear in his obituary.

What follows is from my twenty-year-old memory of a sexual encounter in Phnom Penh on 19 December 1998. I was in a hotel room with a woman who worked out of Martini's, an outdoor bar with large grounds and big screens showing pirated movies. Located around the corner from the Intercontinental Hotel, Martini's had served as a pickup joint during the UNTAC period and continued as a night time venue for years afterwards. It was far enough away from the center of Phnom Penh to maintain the illusion that you were off the grid. The entrance was crowded with parked motorcycles and local beat-up vans. The girls and customers walked in through a narrow entrance, from which they either drifted to a table to join friends or headed for the bar. There were lots of regulars who made an appearance every night. It was a marketplace where survivors of the Khmer Rouge genocide came to sell their bodies.

I found a girl sitting at a table with a couple of friends and we struck up a conversation. Not long afterwards we headed back to my hotel in one of the dodgy vans at the entrance. In the room I switched on the TV and sat on the edge of the bed while she undressed and went into the shower. The channel was tuned to the news, and by the time my companion returned with a towel wrapped around her, the House had begun to vote on the articles of impeachment for William Jefferson Clinton. I looked at the girl. She was about Monica Lewinsky's age. She had no idea what an intern was or even who Bill Clinton was. It was one of those historical moments with my libido winning the war against my intellectual curiosity. It was a perfect Bill moment, positioned between delayed gratification and wanting to eat the whole bag of donuts.

She asked me if there was some music video I could put on. I told her the President of the United States had a problem. She sighed, lobbying again for at least a soap opera as a compromise. It was a cultural divide. This was *The Big Weird*; it had jumped out of the covers of a book and come to life. She massaged my back as I watched the roll call, each representative voting while knowing their constituents were watching and more importantly, their wives.

The massage led to hands covering more and more territory until we were on top of one another. She didn't mind that I continued to watch the votes being tallied on the TV screen. We were already in the future where people fornicated in the present while their minds ran through the memory terminal, hitching a flight to the past. I was enjoying sex while watching an official vote to dislodge the most powerful man in the world from office for lying about sex. Some argue sex has always been the ultimate political act. The history of primates is the struggle for domination and coercion between sex partners.

In Bill Clinton's case, his fling with Monica Lewinsky had become a kind of theatre (apparently he watched the proceeding while on a visit to Israel). It was our soap opera, in which the moralists turned on him like a pack of dogs. Later it turned out a number of the most vocal morality defenders who voted against Clinton had mistresses. It was never about sex; it was about an opportunity for political gain.

The House passed a resolution of impeachment bringing closure to the first stage in the political drama (the Senate later voted to acquit Clinton). The moment had passed. Clinton had officially become part of history, albeit only a few minutes old. I fumbled under the sheets until I found the remote control and with my free hand pointed it like a gun at the TV. Blam. The screen turned blank, and the House, America, and Bill Clinton all vanished, leaving a dead silence.

I didn't say anything. Neither did she. Words are optional tools when it comes to sex. It's not like you need to give directions or ask a lot of questions. We resumed our business like a couple of primates who'd been temporarily stunned with tranquilizer guns. Neither of us focused on the moment. In a queen-size bed. Naked. Bodies coupled together. My mind occupied a seat in the gallery of the House and then the image of Clinton's letter framed on my desk moved past like one of those strange floaters that cross your field of vision. The girl's head was back at the table with her friends at Martini's or maybe planting rice upcountry, or, judging from the frantic movements, running for her life through some forest chased by a cadre. How does anyone measure weirdness? That night in Phnom Penh with a hooker next to me in bed, watching Clinton's wings clipped on TV, qualified as weird enough to keep countless neurons firing up whenever Clinton's name has been mentioned since. We aren't that different from Pavlov's dog. Someone says the word and we can't stop ourselves from drooling.

A Google search revealed a detail that I'd not remembered about the timing. Unless you travel or have global connections, it is easy to forget the time difference between two events. When it comes to digging into our memory about the past, time zone variations between one place and another isn't a high priority. It takes some forensic investigation to confirm the time when comparing two distant places. The date of 19 December 1998 was a Saturday in America. The first article of impeachment was passed by the House at 1:25 p.m. on that Saturday. In Cambodia but it was already Sunday. I watched live on TV with the calendar already flipped to 20 December 1998 as the House voted on 19th December to seal Clinton's fate, adding to the far-flung oddity of the association. Time wise I was in the future watching an historical political event unfold in the past. I watched the vote tally on Article 1 of the impeachment that William Jefferson Clinton willfully provided perjurious, false and misleading testimony to the grand jury concerning his relationship with an intern. He'd lied to a Federal grand jury. There is a lesson here: If Clinton had been working out complicated historical time zone differences, his brain wouldn't have had time to focus on sex. Deliberate thought is a passion killer.

That night in Phnom Penh seems like it happened a long time ago and at the same time as if it were yesterday. Our long-term memories of weirdness have a timeless quality— ruptured a bit if you reflect about the river of history that has flowed through our lives since 1998. Who in December 1998 would have thought that the Republicans who couldn't wait to nail Bill Clinton as a sexual deviant would have no problem in 2016 electing Donald "Grab 'em by the Pussy" Trump as the president of the United States?

How experience and information is loaded into memory, what catches fire and stays in memory, and how we access those memories for political, social, and economic purposes haven't changed. What has changed is a cultural shift. The social media and other the technological advances have narrowed the range and nature of what causes people to pay attention. We experience a different reality now, and in the future, when we look back, our memories will have shifted like tectonic plates creating new continents that never existed in the past.

Some of what shocked our ancestors has lost its power. As we no longer notice an event, a state of affairs, or a person, we won't remember having witnessed it. Over time we've become accustomed to what once had triggered terror and fear—the ingredients to cement a memory in place—such as someone driving a car or flying a plane. We are good at normalizing technological changes. But what becomes normal is also forgettable. It passes us by in the street or in the air and leaves no more of an imprint on our memory than the color of the sun today.

Clinton's impeachment was an unusual event to start with, but in my case it was linked to a personal experience that re-enacted the private moments that Clinton was being raked over the coals for, making it even more memorable to me. A strong connection between the public and private worlds is abnormal, a fluke. But consensual sex in itself is quite normal, and like other pleasures, unless tied to some heightened emotion, loses its place in long-term memory. Clinton is unlikely to be the only president to have received a blowjob in the White House from someone other than his wife. And the impeachment wasn't really about sexual morality so much as it was an early shot fired in the looming civil conflict between America's Old and New People. History records a long list of dead foreigners, barbarians, who killed and fucked their way across Asia and Europe. Such violence was once normal, too. That night in 1998, no one wanted to hear that by historical standards, Bill had a much better sexual record than most popes from the Middle Ages.

Have you ever wanted to go back in time and replay a moment you remember from your past so that you can edit the content based on what you feel and know now? One of the edit reels of my memory is my night with a Martini's freelancer in bed at the Intercontinental Hotel on

19 December 1998, Washington, D.C. time. It is said a man is only as good as his memories. The fact that all of our memories are edited over time is one of the secrets people discover on their own. My new version, as just shared with you, is far more controlled and stripped of willful blindness, with biases rooted out.

The whole scene, of course, is absurd. Not specifically what happened, but the connection as preserved in my memory. What if that woman hadn't gone to Martini's or had rejected my advances, or if I had decided to go out drinking with friends that night? Maybe that day would have passed like the following day or the day after that—days for which I now have no recollection of whom I saw, what I ate, where I went, what book I was reading, or what I experienced. I'm sure I engaged in all of those activities on those other days, but I have no more recollection than I have of 12 February 1999. Those memories didn't stretch the synapses enough to prevent their being purged during that night's sleep. In fact I have no evidence to prove they ever were stored in my memory. I can't Google to find out what I was doing on those days. That means what I experienced is totally and irretrievably lost.

For me, Bill Clinton's impeachment had been the equivalent of a *Simpsons* episode, and I'd been like a kid with a bowl of jellybeans, gorging on sugar. That's why I remember it. But I could have experienced the woman in the hotel room and the historical moment in many other ways. Next to me was a young woman, a contemporary of Monica Lewinsky. I had chosen to put her in a situation infinitely more morally questionable than Clinton had done with his intern. I had seen her in the context of her history. She'd been a young girl at the time of the Khmer Rouge genocide and reign of terror. Anyone who had witnessed those events had experienced a "Guernica moment." The trace of it would be a distant dull glow in her eyes, not quite sadness or grief, caused by ripples of memory from her past that disabled her ability to resist. Sitting on my bed was a human casualty who had stumbled out of Guernica and found a world where she could never be rescued. Nothing that came afterwards could register in her memory with the vividness of those early experiences. Martini's was another kind of refugee camp processing women who had been children in the Khmer Rouge Guernica. She'd gone with me as she'd witnessed others going in silence with their executioners.

Here is my edit, the memory I wish I had. I turn off the TV and Clinton's impeachment and ask her about her childhood. She tells me a story, which is a variation of Sam Sotha's story. Even in our memory edits we reach for stock scenes to fill in the gaps. I find myself tumbling into her tiny, dimpled side pocket of a local universe. The life of that time had become normal, with less terror and fear each day she'd survived until one day it had become normal, and that had marked the day that Year Zero had started for her and others like her.

Pablo Picasso painted his *Guernica* as a set of images that encrypted death and suffering. His painting of the Spanish Civil War was a surreal shout: "This should never be normal. Remember this!" And he passed the painting to posterity no doubt believing that his message was pristine and clear, that everyone who saw it had the key to unlock its meaning. But time passes and we forget the past, individually and collectively, and lose the key to open the meanings of works of art.

Only a select few have the experience and knowledge to decode the original horror depicted in Picasso's painting. I'm not one of the select few. I intellectually know *Guernica* as a painting but I don't have emotional knowledge of it at the deepest level. In my memory redo, my edit, when I look into the eyes of the Martini's freelancer, I can see she is a person of emotional intelligence, so she must be one of those select few. I have beside me on the bed a peasant girl who knows infinitely more about the art of terror and fear than I could ever know. No foreigner has asked her about her past until tonight. She's never been asked about her personal knowledge. Foreigners have no frame of reference from which to ask at the emotional level. Such things don't happen in the Simpsons' world. Homer, Marge, Bart, Lisa, and Maggie have personal problems whose perimeters are neatly set. Picasso painted a scene that would be alien to their memory, a cartoon memory that they would assume everyone shares.

Bill and I had something in common: we suffered a kind of Asperger's syndrome in reading the woman we wanted to engage in sex with. It was a blindness that prevents each new generation from receiving the emotionally charged content that had shaped the memories of the dead generations that preceded it—dead artists, dead people and animals, a time of life buried in dusty history books and captured in paintings.

My frame of reference for interpreting interactions, nonverbal gestures, and expressions draws from a modern context. The events that excited the emotions in the past, those are gone, and the trail of facts, photos, paintings, books, and films that have followed are the only records of events for most of us. But the day-to-day emotional ups and downs, the sense of fear and terror shaped by those events and that technology are mostly gone. We can only speculate from the artifacts what they must have felt, and how their emotional lives were warped. The time is approaching when there are no longer among the living those with direct experience of the Holocaust or the Spanish Civil War. In fifty years that will happen for the Khmer Rouge genocide period. With no living person left to remember the emotions, a cultural Asperger's barrier falls between the living and the dead. We see what they saw, at least in bits and pieces, but we don't feel what they felt. Our empathy is mainly for the living; there isn't enough supply to nurture the dead.

That was a lesson I wished I'd learned in 1998. Such knowledge would have saved me from a lot of mistakes. The expat life I was a part of overlapped with pockets of local culture and history, but the two worlds rarely connected in deeper ways. The cultural universe isn't isotropic. It is dimpled with small, wild, impenetrable areas, natural habitats, walled off into encrypted jungles that follow no logic and make no rational sense. As outsiders marooned inside that expat world, we caught the faint outlines of those other lives, frozen in illegible blocks of time from which, even with the best hammer and chisel, we could sculpt only rough approximations of the real heartbeat of horror and fear into our outsiders' narratives. My attention was on Bill Clinton as I lived that moment detached from the history of the person next to me in bed—a primate moment, as one alpha primate watched another being taken down by the colony over a sexual transgression.

Our memory system is a primate artifact. Usually we ignore it. We seek to transcend it. Our best counterfactual authors, like Philip K. Dick and Philip Roth, confirm that nothing in our memory of the world is stable or certain. Change a detail in the past and the present is a foreign land. No outcome is preordained. If Monica Lewinsky had dry-cleaned her dress and not poured out her heart to a friend, the TV at my hotel would have run a local soap opera on 19 December 1998, and that day would have been no different from 20 or 21 December. No impeachment would have entered the history books. For me no memory of an unusual sexual encounter would have been recorded.

Memory Manifesto

No matter how many times I learn this lesson, I discover that I must learn it again. It is difficult to accept how much of what we remember is tied to accidents and the whims behind events. Rewind the tape and the event changes, the memories are altered, and we wouldn't know the difference between what happened, what might have happened, and what could happen on the replay.

EIGHTTEEN

Sitting in my room at the Lux Hotel in 2017, I wondered if Bill Clinton ever got around to reading *The Big Weird*. If he did, then he would have understood about the "sickness"—in an El Dorado search for a sexual Utopia—that infected so many men who came to Southeast Asia in those years. Maybe he thought, as most expats did, that he was immune. The sickness would never capture him. He had his memories, and I had mine. Since then Bill Clinton had become an old man, white-haired, haggard, shoulders slumped, his lips moving like one of those disturbed, blanket-wrapped people I passed in New York on Canal or Grand Street in the early 1980s. It was as if he were talking to himself as he tried to remember what had happened, where he was, and when his life had taken a sharp turn and gone off the rails.

As I wrote those words, I asked myself whether I might have turned into one of those muttering old men myself. If so, who was I addressing my words to, and who was listening? Why talk about any of this? Why not leave the sleeping dogs snoring on the semen-stained dress? That's what memory does to us; it forces us to go through incidents again and again, and before you know it, what you remember is jumbled up with what you want to remember. You can't Google to fill in forgotten details, the ones your memory refuses to give up. Other, unwanted details float to the top of the stew pot of your personal historical archive, and those stick to you like a jealous lover. With Asperger's a person often assumes a literal interpretation of an interaction because he or she is unable to read its emotional subtext. Bill and I share a different kind of distortion that is really a deception. We are guilty because we were perfectly capable of reading and understanding the subtext of a power imbalance behind a vulnerable woman's submission to events, but consciously we refused to do so. We placed a higher priority on our pleasure.

The hourglass is running down for Bill Clinton and the rest of us from his generation. We sit looking at the remaining stock of sand, thinking the same thought—ain't much left—and picking up a book to remind us of some piece of wisdom we wished had lodged in our memories thirty years ago. We greedily consume the insights from Socrates to Camus that, if we had read them earlier and understood them deeply, might have changed the course of our lives. With not much sand left to fall, we become frantic to store as much wisdom as we can before the hourglass empties and the bottom of the glass signals time has stopped for us. No amount of sleep rescales that hourglass. All of our memories eventually fall into the bottom, and the next generation turns the glass over, making the same mistake of waiting to the end before reading the books we neglected. The original sin wasn't giving us fire; it was giving us language and a way to record our memories in books without giving us the attention necessary both to read and to map our lives from our reading.

Language is the tool we use to unclog the drainpipe that connects us to our distant past. We sense a tsunami of information entered that drainpipe but what comes out in our lifetime is a filtered drip that soon evaporates in the heat of present worries and preoccupations. What we receive from the past wets our appetite but doesn't quench our thirst. We are constantly reminded of the vast sea of lost and forbidden information that is beyond our grasp. Where, for example, is the information about the inner emotional life of slaves owned by the slaveholders who wrote the American constitution? What was the life of the mind of the Khmer slaves that built Angkor Wat?

We are doomed to live in the present with only a rough understanding of the events, thoughts, feelings, and people from the past. Where they killed people and why are lost except in the few surviving writings we believe are divining rods to locate the time and place of those acts and motives. We fail to appreciate that what drives our emotions also flows through our own clogged drainage system from the unconscious to the conscious mind. Time and technology erase the past memories, dreams and fears. We are no longer afraid of a man on a horse, or the sight of a car. We can't resist making our own emotional maps from the scraps of gossip, rumors, and the constant drumbeat of entertaining jokesters.

NINETEEN

In 1984 I was a law professor in Canada on sabbatical leave. A New York publisher had accepted my first novel, *His Lordship's Arsenal*. Like many young writers, I read this first acceptance as an omen. I left my tenured position to devote myself to writing novels full-time, a decision that made little sense to my family and friends. But I was determined to become a literary man. New York was the place to chase that dream. I'd had the cloistered experience of a professor when I arrived in New York City. My literary hero, who came from a similar background, was Jorge Luis Borges. I set my sights high but not that high. I was the kind of writer who needed to experience life before I could write about it. My mental vault was stacked with the sort of semantic memory one would expect of a law professor. But my episodic memory shelves looked more like Europe after the Black Death—depopulated and barren.

I found this missing experience on the back streets of Brooklyn, where the poor scammed, sold drugs, organized themselves into gangs and mugged, bullied, and shot each other in parks, schoolyards, alleys, and projects. The 1980s was a happening time on those streets. My luck turned for the better when I received official permission from the NYPD to ride as a civilian observer. I managed to gain permission through the old-boy system. An ex-student of mine at the law school of the University of Leicester, John Stevens (a London cop who was on sabbatical leave to teach at John Jay College of Criminal Justice and who later rose through the ranks to become commissioner of Scotland Yard), made the arrangements. John had invited me to stay as a guest at his apartment near Studio 54 in midtown New York. On a gloomy, rainy night in Vancouver, I phoned him and told him that I was on my way.

John changed my life by his invitation and later by making a couple of phone calls on my behalf to the NYPD. I was a Canadian and he was English, and we had cracked the American blue wall. I can't imagine that happening today. During those early days in New York, John taught me that running circles around someone with legal arguments had its place, but the real game was cultivating and maintaining the right network of connections. You were either in or out of the loop. John was on the inside track. The word went down the line, and I was suddenly in the loop, or a tiny piece of it.

My experience from riding with the cops came mainly from the back of a cruiser patrolling the poorer quarters of Brooklyn. In the early 1980s those areas were vast, scary, dangerous blocks of projects and slums. I witnessed the lives of the residents through the eyes of the police. The midwife at the birth of Vincent Calvino was John Stevens. He eased me into a squad car with two cops from the 68th Precinct— one Hispanic, the other Arab—and we set off from 11:00 p.m. to 6:00 a.m., taking calls through the night.

That old New York has vanished. It exists still in the memory of those of us who lived there on streets controlled by gangs, drug dealers, and thugs. In those days you made your bones the first time someone shot at you. For me it happened one night when we were on patrol in Brooklyn. I sat in the back; the two uniformed cops sat up front. A sedan drove straight at us. The driver flashed his high beams at us. Alvarez, who was driving, stopped the cruiser and turned on the red flashing light. A man and a woman emerged from the other car, leaving the engine idling while blocking our cruiser. Alvarez swung open the squad car door and, without a word, eased himself out; his partner had already engaged the man and woman in conversation. I stepped out of the cruiser and stood beside it watching the two uniforms casually talking to the two civilians as if they were old friends.

They turned out to be a two-person team of undercover NYPD cops, working in Brooklyn on a drug bust. Alvarez knew both of them. The headlights of the cruiser illuminated the male team member as he brushed back his jacket, revealing a handgun holstered below his left armpit. It looked like an unintentional act. There was nothing to indicate he was reaching for his gun. But on a dark Brooklyn street I felt nervous. Something didn't seem quite right. It was a gut feeling. Today those streets are neighborhoods filled with hipsters. But then the resident subculture was heavily armed.

Alvarez said, "Come over here, let me introduce you. This is the law professor," he said. "He's riding with us."

At that moment someone took a couple of quick shots at us. The gunfire came from a roof or window of one of the surrounding buildings. We were standing in a canyon of projects. It was impossible to identify the position of the shooter. No one was hit. Guns were drawn. I knelt beside the squad car. The two uncover cops hunched down, knees on the ground, scanning the surrounding buildings. It was two in the morning. Lights came on in a number of windows. The four cops and I waited for the shooter to adjust his sights and take another shot. Exposed as we were, we would have been easy to pick off. But another shot never came. After a couple of minutes everyone was back on their feet, saying goodbye and moving back to their cars. None of the cops appeared shaken by the incident.

Alvarez and his partner grinned at me. "They were just fucking with us," said Alvarez, who was studying to pass his sergeant's examination the next week. It was no big deal. After the shift ended, I noticed they failed to write up the incident. When I asked why they'd not reported it, they shrugged. It would involve too much paperwork to file a report over a couple of isolated shots. A report meant a couple of hours of paperwork and talking to superiors. Alvarez had an examination to study for, and his partner had a girlfriend waiting for him in a warm bed.

I understood later their real reason for ignoring the shots. Both men would have been teased to death by their colleagues: "Hey, Alvarez, whatever happened to the lone gunman? Could it have been the Lone Ranger?" Or even worse, "What kind of narcissist are you, Alvarez? What makes you think they were shooting at you? More likely they were shooting at some bullshit gang over some bullshit piece of territory." Except no NYPD I knew in 1985 would have used a ten-dollar word like "narcissist." It was that kind of word said to the wrong guy in Brooklyn that got you shot for real. He'd just assume you'd called him an asshole.

It was only the young law professor from Canada who thought this was a big deal. For the others, shot at once, well, "Shit, that's part of the job." More accurately, rather than being shot at, I happened to be on a street in Brooklyn when shots were fired. Who knows who the shooter was aiming at? Looking back on the incident now, I wonder what gave me lifetime bragging rights about surviving a sniper in the bowels of a noir part of New York? The incident wouldn't lodge in the memory of my riding companions. They'd heard gunshots far too many times to remember all of them.

But I would never forget that moment. There's something about a canyon of high-rise slums that amplifies the sound of gunfire—the violence echoes off the windows and walls like the sound of a cathedral bell.

Riding with the NYPD, I learned a few things about the world of policing, the culture of police, the real dangers they faced, and the shitty pay they received. You didn't get inside their club easily. They eyed outsiders as people who could only cause them trouble and put them in greater danger. The NYPD officers I knew had a casual way of dealing with death, injuries, and childbirth. It was how they survived emotionally. Once we were walking through the morgue and there was a body on a gurney pushed against a wall in the corridor. Alvarez stopped and looked at the dead man. There was a jagged black bullet hole in his forehead. Alvarez checked the toe tag. "Shit, I hadn't seen Waldo for a week. I wondered where he'd gone." And he walked off down the corridor, talking about a football game he was trying to get tickets for.

TWENTY

The memories of my NYPD experiences returned to the forefront of my thoughts in 2006 when I went in the field with a team of the UN-supported Cambodian landmine personnel. Like John Stevens before him, a Cambodian named Sam Sotha had connections. He was the big boss and made the necessary arrangements for me to tag along as a civilian observer. For me this connection, like the NYPD one, was a fluke. Sam and I shared a mutual friend named Richard Diran, a talented photographer, painter, and gem dealer. Richard insisted that I meet Sam and Sony, his wife, and arranged a luncheon at their house. They had a villa in Phnom Penh, and Sony and a maid had prepared a lavish lunch for Richard and me. The table was set with real silver cutlery and china plates and bowls of tossed salad, vegetables, chicken, and pasta.

Over the course of our lunch Sam and Sony told me their story. Through a series of improbable escapes the two had survived four years living in a number of different Khmer forced labor camps. They had watched as people they knew were taken away and killed. They witnessed the brutality of the Khmer Rouge every day for all of those years. Around their camps the killing fields spread out in an ever-growing mass boneyard. After the refugee camps that followed those years, Sam and his wife had settled in

California, where Sam became politically active in the local Cambodian community. He had thrived in the milieu of American politics. With those political skills he had found his talents in demand by the post-Khmer Rouge government led by Hun Sen.

Sam had originally been appointed as head of the Cambodian Mine Action Authority, the agency in charge of landmine clearance for the entire country. Questions were raised that spilled over into a controversy about finances and management during his tenure, but nothing came of it. Hun Sen decided to appoint him to head a newly formed government agency: the National Regulatory Authority on Mine Action, with the responsibility for clearing all landmines in the country. The unfortunate acronym of the new agency was NRA. This NRA had a huge job ahead of it.

Sometime after our luncheon, I visited Sam in his office. Sam's office was on the third floor of an old French colonial building that had a layout and style that managed to combine the best features of a prison and a military hospital. I climbed several flights of marble stairs and walked down a long corridor to the director's office. Smiling to see me from behind his desk, he crossed the room and embraced me. He walked among cases displaying dozens of deactivated landmines, proving that an impressive range of ordnance had been buried in the ground to blow off legs or kill with a messy, bloody efficiency. Each of the landmines was displayed with a card with the manufacturer's name and country of origin. That was a nice touch, I thought. Walking a donor who was a citizen of one of those countries to the display case would have turned the guilt knobs of conscience. Donors promised money, atonement payments for their fellow citizens' part in profiting from supplying the war machine on all sides. The little notes in the display case were a kind of memory token, a currency used to impress allies inside governments and international relief agencies.

I had gone to Sam's office to talk about the details of my field trip with one of the teams sent out to find and dispose of landmines. As we discussed the plans, Sam pointed at a large detailed map on the wall behind his desk. It showed the minefields that had been cleared and ones yet to be cleared with colored pins. Most of the map was covered with red pins, marking the places not yet cleared. Given a rate of clearance of ten square kilometers a year, the map indicated it would take around three hundred years to complete the mission. The official estimates ranged between six and ten million landmines.

Finding the landmines was a weird kind of Fermi paradox—which questions why extraterrestrials, if they are indeed out there (as the math suggests they must be), haven't contacted us. With landmines, we know they are there, but they will never contact us; we must find them. In those years figuring where those landmines were placed required a Herculean act of individual and collective memory organizing. The landmines had been laid down under the rule of several governments, including forces loyal to Lon Nol's regime of the early 1970s.

Those who had done the landmine placement hadn't bothered to leave systematic written records of their work. In the Khmer Rouge era that was New People thinking, and you could get yourself killed for less. But it wasn't just the Khmer Rouge who laid mines. None of the forces planting them had any consensus about grids, geometry, or measurement; they left no maps, books, memos, or photographs. However, many of the mines had been planted under the supervision of people from the area. As in ancient times, locals knew the lay of the land by a rock, a tree, a bush, or some other physical attribute. Such landmarks, often impermanent, were the only points of reference. It was pre-book kind of memory, the old kind that was confined to the synapses and neurons inside a living person's head.

It was as if a medieval mentality had taken charge for a few years, with every region and district going its own way, and decades later the freed serfs were sent into the field to remember their long-ago works. One of the costs of the resulting gap in collective memory can be quantified—this lethal war technology had blown off approximately forty thousand legs over a three-decade period. Even as late as 2016 twenty people were killed and twenty-nine injured by landmines in Cambodia.

Given the history of the landmines, how does anyone go about finding millions of them many years later, when memories of the witnesses have faded? Maybe planting the first mine would have been memorable, but after weeks, months, and years of planting them, individual placements must have become as memorable as bolts tightened on an assembly line. That is a memory problem. I wanted to go in the field to find out what mental hacks and workarounds the Cambodian demining crews were using to find the mines—and to return to Phnom Penh without having a leg blown off.

I'd asked Sam, "Since the teams don't know where the mines are, what is the number of casualties?"

Sam had smiled. He'd likely heard this question asked many times by UN officials, the Swedes who funded sniffer dogs, and a long list of NGOs who sought to help in the effort.

"We are careful."

He could see I wasn't happy with the answer, but I let it pass.

"You'll see. Ask me again once you are back."

"These guys aren't using amulets and lucky numbers, are they, Sam?"

"That's Thailand mine clearing. We use modern techniques," he replied, slipping into the chair behind his desk. "Don't worry, my men will look after you. Stay close to the team. Don't wander off. You'll be okay."

This sounded like what I imagined a Californian politician said to gain the confidence of a voter. I was in for the field trip.

I said, "Okay, Sam, we'll talk later."

I had no intention of wandering off into a Cambodian minefield on my own. In Sam's world, a person only had safety inside the group. Once you broke free, that's when you were injured or worse. I trusted Sam as I'd read his manuscript by then and knew what he'd been through. Actually, my concern for personal safety made me feel ashamed. I hadn't signed on for a temple tour; I'd asked to go into the minefields. But there I was in Sam's office feeling unsafe, seeking assurances, and looking at the sea of red pins on the wall map. If I couldn't muster the courage to spend a week in the field with a professional crew of demining personnel, maybe I should accept that I wasn't cut out for the fieldwork of life and just crawl back to a teaching post.

Sam and Sony's story of their four years in Khmer Rouge forced labor camps was inspiring, but it also gave me the feeling that no matter what I did, where I went, or what I saw, nothing I did could come close to matching the intensity of their experiences. In the grand scheme of things, I was a novice, a tourist, a voyeur who could bail out the moment things turned ugly. Most people on earth are more like Sam and Sony in those years of suffering, with no control over their lives and no options.

One day Sam had showed me his handwritten account of their four years inside the Khmer Rouge gulag. He's had an inmate of his refugee camp draw illustrations for the book. Both the author and the illustrator had escaped the Khmer Rouge, and Sam's book was a kind of Khmer Guernica project to capture the destruction of that time. The manuscript recounted Sam and Sony's brushes with death time after time. It was as if they'd been caught up in a hellish version of the *Groundhog Day* film. The story was powerful and haunting. After reading Sam's harrowing account of their four years in the forced labor camps, I came away in awe that they'd survived. How do some people endure experiences like heaps of bodies piled next to their camp and not go insane? After reading the manuscript, I believed that others who ask such questions should read Sam's firsthand account. I ultimately arranged for the book to be published in 2007 as *In the Shade of a Quiet Killing Place*.

Sam and Sony had pretty much seen the worst kind of organized evil their fellow humans were capable of visiting upon the innocent. Sam had agreed to embed me with his demining team as they traveled upcountry on assignment. I felt the only way to understand something about the memory of the Khmer time was to join the search for what had been left behind and forgotten.

My time in the NYPD patrol car had prepared me for the suspicions that members of the demining team would inevitably have about the insertion of a day-tripper into their serious business. The last thing anyone in a field of danger wants is to babysit someone who is connected to the big boss. What everyone expects from this sort of situation is a show-and-tell tour that advertises the competence of the officials producing the show. What made New York different was that after a couple of months the show runners exhausted their standard material and I saw the reality of the job: long stretches of stupidity, mindless gossip, and boredom occasionally interrupted by moments of absolute terror.

For most of the New People—and I included myself in that category—thoughts about violence were an intellectual parlor game. But in the field that logic broke apart. The violence wasn't just in the head. You saw what the violence did to your blood rate with your adrenal gland pumping you up. The formal logic was buried when that happened. You ran on pure emotions. All those carefully made plans, hours of indoctrination and training, and the morality your mother taught you evaporated in the heat-baking panic moment when you had to make a split-second decision to survive. Later, when you have to testify in a witness box about what you remember, your memory tries to make sense of what was an instinctive, automatic reaction. Quick action in the field, or to use Daniel Kahneman's *Thinking, Fast and Slow* template, Stage 1 thinking, must later be justified as if it had been Stage 2 deliberative thinking. The justice system judges your actions not by putting itself in your emotional space when you did something but by reference to a very different way of thinking that can only occur when emotions have cooled and the dust has settled. That shift from Stage 1 action to Stage 2 accountability was something that New People did to undermine Old People.

The demining team I was assigned to had five members. Two of the men had fought for the Lon Nol regime, two were ex-Khmer Rouge, and the team leader had a mysterious history that straddled both horses. He was the only one who spoke English, so he acted as my interpreter as we headed upcountry in a white Land Rover. The roads were overgrown water buffalo trails, and the Land Rover would flatten the tall elephant grass as we roared through.

At the end of a half-hour drive we pulled into a clearing. A man waited inside a Russian tractor with a bulldozer blade on the front. He'd parked off to the side of the road. The sound of our vehicle must have awakened him because he had the telltale sleep crease on the right side of his face that matched the pattern of the snakeskin cover on the back of his seat. As the group gathered around the bulldozer, the driver jumped down, all smiles to see us, or perhaps it was a sliver of his dream that accounted for the grin.

After a brief exchange, the driver climbed back into his seat and slowly moved the bulldozer forward ten meters into a thicket of underbrush. The driver sat in a protected cage, and the bulldozer's blade was manufactured to absorb the shock of an explosion from a landmine or unexploded ordnance (UXO). The blade struck the underbrush as if it were a brick wall. The team leader and I followed behind while the other members of the team stayed in the Land Rover. For about fifteen minutes we watched as the bulldozer backed up, assaulted the undergrowth, bounced back on its huge tires, and roared forward again, making only a couple of meters of progress.

"When he hits a mine, the blade protects him," explained the leader.

"How many landmines has he found today?" I asked.

The team leader smiled and shrugged as if I'd asked a stupid question. It was the kind of question a law professor would ask. Standing in the field with the team members, I was as far away from a law classroom as I could get. The non-logic of violence that had been used by the Old People to hide the landmines and UXOs was useless in locating them decades later. Propaganda had been used to hide the mines, and it was no surprise that propaganda played an important role in the effort to recover them. By the time we were back in the Land Rover, I understood that what I'd witnessed was part of a script. It was how officials showed off their equipment and manpower to foreigners who would in turn pass the hat among the Westerners who knew their governments and corporations had secretly left their fingerprints on millions of mines still buried in Cambodia.

I swallowed hard and sat in silence as the Land Rover turned around. We drove to the next destination without further discussing what we'd seen. This wasn't what I'd expected or wanted. I felt like a Western law professor who'd been invited to witness an old Soviet show trial so he could compliment the organizers on their sense of decorum and justice. At the next stop I was treated to the sight of a German shepherd trained to locate mines. As I recall it was a gift of Swedish donors who were keen on the canine solution to the mine problem. The dog found nothing in the thirty minutes I was watching it work under a baking sun. Later it was given water and allowed to stretch out in the shade. One of the deminers said that dogs were of limited use. There was too much dust, they got overheated in the overhead sun, and the bush was too dense for them to get their snouts to the ground. In other words, the dogs looked right for the Hollywood part of mine detectors, but if mine detection were left to dogs, rather than three hundred years to clear all the mines in Cambodia, the task would take closer to a thousand. Since then I've read that rats have been trained to do the job with far more efficiency than dogs, but rats don't make the A-list (with the exception of *Stuart Little*) of animals starring in a Hollywood film.

That night at dinner we all sat around a table drinking cold beer. You might think that a drinking session on the edge of minefields with a group of men in uniform who are speaking a language you don't understand could be nothing more than entertaining. In fact the evenings around the table revealed more to me about the deeper problems of mine clearance than my time in the field, proving to be a time of enlightenment about the nature of violence and the actors involved, and what it means to clean up the weapons of violence after an orgy of mass killing. After a few drinks, the men opened up and swapped stories about when they were young. The old days had their eyes misting over. (As I write this I remember the GI from Maine who wanted to start a second-hand auto parts business in Saigon.) They talked about where they'd been stationed and what they'd been doing, though the ex-Khmer Rouge didn't speak of bashing any heads. But all of the men around the table had experience in planting landmines. It was their karma to return in search of what they and others like them had once planted.

After a few nights this experience in mine planting was revealed to be a major qualification for the job of demining. It made good sense—hire the guys who hid the mines to dig them up. Each night the team would make decisions for the next day based on what they remembered that evening: distance, location, landscape details. The team leader would keep notes. We'd go back to an area where they'd soldiered years before. In those days they'd been trying to kill each other. No dogs, rats, or Russian tractors with bulldozer blades attached. In 2006 they sat around a table remembering together. Memory was all they had, but memory was fallible. The frustration of using an unreliable memory to map your way through a minefield was only exceeded by the fear of its potential danger. Memory's metaphor was the bulldozer blade hitting an invisible wall, bouncing off as the whole Russian tractor shuddered before reversing the gears and trying again. And again.

Memories of past mine-planting had a similar operational feature. One member of the team would put down his beer and begin to talk with a degree of conviction about where some mines had been laid. Others would sit silently, listening to the buzz of the conversation, drinking, thinking, and remembering how on other nights no one had said anything about how similar memories hadn't panned out. Those memories of their youth, when their brains were at their peak for laying down memories, had failed them, knocked them back like the underbrush refusing to yield to the bulldozer. One night the team discussed a field where one of them remembered a sector of a minefield from a couple of small trees. When they went to the field, he couldn't find those trees. He scanned a horizon with only tall trees. Were these the same ones grown large? Or was he standing in a different section of the field? Nothing in nature stays static. The paths, the fields, the underbrush, the trees, the villages—all had evolved, leaving behind memories that were isolated artifacts like pinned butterflies in a museum case.

They relied on all they had—their memory. There must at one time have been some maps, records, charts, or diagrams to go by, but if they existed, no one remembered where they'd been stored. Amnesia is the term for a substantial loss of memory. Cambodia after the fall of the Khmer Rouge entered an extended period of collective amnesia. The beer at night jiggled the synapses, releasing a chemical to unlock neurons, and before anyone could say duck, they were back in the past, much younger versions of themselves, digging a hole to lay a mine. But instead of finding memory maps of the mine locations, they found memory holes. The process was like what I imagine fact-checking the Bible would have been like around a table of a small handful of the original authors whose paycheck depended on convincing others their memories made them reliable witnesses. A lesson for me from those evenings and the days that followed was that no one in the field talks about alt-facts and minefields in the same sentence. You can claim to have your own facts and assert that they are as valid as the contrary facts claimed by others. You are welcome to take that attitude with you when you try to find and clear minefields. I wish you good luck.

My experience with the deminers, none of whom had much formal education, hammered home that modern weapons have a definitive reality, one demarcated with sharp boundary lines that are unforgiving to those who refuse to believe they exist. What bonded the team was their shared capacity to forget. They'd been no older than boys when they'd planted the landmines or UXOs. But when you are walking through a field that you only half-recall planting mines in, you are converted to the importance of precise recall of details. Fuzzy memories are more dangerous than a total absence of recall. The collective memory of Cambodia had big holes as if it had gone to sleep and the synapses had been flushed of essential information. What filled in the resulting space were feelings—regret, remorse, and the desire for revenge.

Until the ghosts of those feelings were appeased, there could never be reconciliation. The memory of the nation's past must be aligned, agreed upon, and accepted no matter where the chips fell. That's what made reconciliation of the past hard. Each side wants the chips to land on the side of what they remember happening, a memory that gives them a winning hand. The Cambodian conflict over memory was a post-fighting war that has lasted far longer than the physical combat. Cambodians have tried but have largely failed to reconcile conflicting memories of what happened in the past. If you can't agree on what happened, or where you left the landmines, you will spend decades surrounding the problem without getting any closer to a resolution.

There are consequences to reconciliation; someone takes the responsibility for actions that caused suffering. One group's memory will be right; the other group's memory will be wrong. Black and white, the two colors available, are insufficient choices to portray a gray world when color mixing isn't possible. When group violence has resulted in widespread murder, it is difficult to get individuals to step forward and admit they were the ones who swung the ax, shot the rifle, laid the landmines. In their minds it wasn't them; it was the other group possessed by evil that did the murdering.

TWENTY-ONE

Getting former combatants who'd once fought one another to sit around a table in the minefields to remember was not just a start; it was the only viable option. The war crimes trials that began five years later in Phnom Penh were another attempt by a handful of people, culled from a cast of thousands, at collective remembering. A skeptic might call it selective remembering, noting that the push to forget the larger context of how it had all happened was what drove the process forward. It has always been much easier to pin the blame for genocide on a handful of ex-leaders than on the larger group responsible for it. As this group numbered in the millions, arresting and trying a few of the elderly leaders would have to do. Hun Sen's view that an expansion of the investigation into the larger group of officials and officers would deliver the nation back into civil war may have had some validity.

The problem with rumors as a basis for planning a demining operation mirrored the larger problem of rumors in Cambodian daily life. This way of thinking to solve a problem was one of the more persistent holdovers from the Khmer Rouge years. If you didn't have the facts handy, rumors would flash out of holsters like guns at the O.K. Corral. Rumors incited violence, hatred, and fear. For the demining teams some of those rumors caused domestic suspicions. One evening around twilight I had a walk outside our camp, looking around and trying to get a sense of the land and the people. Directly across the road was a matronly Cambodian woman in a wrap-around dress and sandals, holding a bunch of leafy green vegetables. This wasn't the time of day for customers to stop along the road to buy produce. From the look of the road, it was never the time to sell goods there. I peered at her motionless form as she stood like a sentry on the road, watching our encampment. She saw me but made no effort to acknowledge my presence or to pretend she was looking at someone else. Apparently, even in the twilight she could tell I wasn't a customer. When I returned inside, I asked Kimsan, the team leader, about the woman on the road.

"Oh, her? That's Chan. She's the wife of Utey."

Utey was one of the demining team members. Kimsan didn't seem upset or surprised about the presence of the woman who obviously was watching the camp entrance.

"What she's doing standing outside?"

"Taking her watch for the others," he replied, enjoying my growing state of confusion.

I took a moment to figure out why Kimsan was grinning.

"Why should she be watching? What is she looking for?"

"Local women trying to sneak into the camp."

I was accustomed to enigmatic explanations in Southeast Asia. Clarity of thought and speech could be a dangerous choice, boxing you into a position, and you were never sure which way the wind would blow tomorrow. But Kimsan had given me enough rope that I decided to go ahead and hang myself.

"Utey's got a girlfriend in the neighborhood?"

The paranoia of the Khmer Rouge hadn't died out. It had become a camp follower of the demining teams. Only, as it turned out, it wasn't paranoia. It turned that out a fairly high percentage of the demining squad had accumulated a string of local wives. By Cambodian standards, with their $168 a month pay from the UN, they were rich. That meant they could support more than one family. They might not remember where they'd planted the landmines in the old days, but they hadn't forgotten the local women, who treated them like rock stars. Their wives had got wind that their wayward husbands in the field were toiling under a hot sun and then returning to camp and the cool embrace of a young woman.

Chan, the woman outside, was taking her turn on guard duty. The wives of the men inside the camp rotated as sentries outside. One of the wives would be across the road watching at all times. Under that bunch of green vegetables she'd be clutching a nasty machete to chase away any local women waiting for a chance to sneak inside and become part of the gravy train that ran through the old killing fields. I can't confirm as fact what one member of the team told me, that at night their wives would ring the camp with landmines so none of the hopeful minor wives would risk losing a leg to infiltrate the camp through the backdoor. If that rumor was true, it closed the circle: men digging up landmines for a good living, and their wives planting landmines around their men to keep competitors away. The men's memories might have been compromised by time, but the memories of their wives, fed by a mixture of rumors and truth, were made of stronger stuff.

The collateral damage of unlocated and unexploded landmines worked its way through unexpected avenues. The violence industry had gone into peacetime operation. Deminers drank beer and exposed gaping holes in their wartime memories, while outside, their wives organized themselves into a new class of prison guards. Road shows of mine fields, sniffer dogs, trained rats, armored Russian tractors, and red signs printed on cardboard with a skull and crossbones demarcating an uncleared field—all of these things persist in my memory. But the sight of the landmine clearance official's wife at twilight in a dusty patch of upcountry Cambodia, holding her hidden machete, ever vigilant, wasn't planned for the tour. It was an unscheduled stop, one you're not supposed to see, and, of course, that is the one that you never forget. If you truly want to remember comings and goings and keep track, a panopticon of jealous wives is a template as old as the species.

TWENTY-TWO

You remember 2007. Of course you do. The Oscar for Best Picture went to *The Departed*; the Nobel Prize for Literature was awarded to Doris Lessing; the Grammy Award for Album of the Year was given for the Dixie Chicks' *Taking the Long Way*; and 2007 was the year that Kurt Vonnegut died, as did David Halberstam and Boris Yeltsin. That's the tip of the iceberg of benchmark events of that year that most people no longer remember.

In 2007 I was back in Phnom Penh with Richard Diran for the launch of Sam's book, *In the Shade of a Quiet Killing Field*. I'd helped Sam come up with the title. It turned out the book was something of a milestone. While there had been other books written by Cambodians about their experiences in forced labor camps, Sam's position as a high-ranking official in the government meant his book received wider media attention in Cambodia. The impact of a book depends on whether it is widely read and influences the opinions of the educated elites. It may take a long time before such influences appear.

Sam's book launch became a big social event. I wore a suit and tie for the occasion. Richard wore his usual rumpled shirt and cargo pants. Around one in the afternoon, Richard and I were ready for lunch. We turned up at Happy Herb

Pizza near the Foreign Correspondents' Club and situated across from the quay.

The waiter came to our table and handed us menus.

"I feel like the large pepperoni," said Richard.

"We can split it," I suggested.

Richard motioned for the waiter to move in closer.

"I want extra happy on the pizza," he whispered.

The waiter smiled at Richard, "How much happy?"

He spoke in a normal voice. He saw no need to whisper about happy toppings on the house pizzas.

"Two dollars of extra happy," said Richard. "And bring us two Tiger beers. Man, I am thirsty. And this launch is starting to make me nervous. Sam's got lots of press to come. He said something about me speaking. I told him, 'Hey, Sam, I'm no good at public speaking.' But he said, 'It don't matter. Just say whatever you want.' " Richard lit a cigarette from one that had burnt down to the end. He sucked hard on the new one in one heroic inhalation. I thought, "Two dollars of happy. How much harm could that do?"

We had lots of time before our appointment to meet Sam. The NRA director for all of Cambodia and his book launch were a good three hours away. Two dollars of extra happiness seemed like a reasonable splurge. Richard was uncomfortable attending public events, especially when there were going to be TV people present plus generals, government officials, and their wives and consorts, who would be decked out in their Imelda Marcos pyramids of raven black hair, jewelry, and designer finery. That kind of event starts like a small brush fire, and soon the whole forest is up in flames. Sam's book launch had become a huge social occasion that just happened to use a book launch as a way for the influential and powerful to mix.

"Man, I hate crowds," said Richard, downing a second piece of the pizza.

The waiter came by our table. "Happy enough?"

Richard gave him a thumbs-up. "Bring me a little more happy, okay?"

After the waiter moved on, he said, "I don't feel anything. I think we've been ripped off. How about you? Do you feel anything?"

"Happy takes time," I said.

"That should be on a T-shirt," Richard said. This statement was followed by his first genuine happy laugh.

"I'd wait before putting more happy on the pizza," I said.

He shrugged as the waiter returned with a ketchup bottle of happy and watched as Richard sprinkled more on the pizza.

"I'd say forget it," said Richard, "but I owe it to Sam to be there for him. He's a friend. He expects me to and so does Sony. What am I gonna say—'Sorry, Sam, I had another appointment?' "

He laughed again and, pulling another cigarette from his pack, lit it up.

"Do you remember the old Russian market in the early '90s?" he asked.

My memory of the Russian market was of a dusty, old-fashioned third-world outdoor market, crammed with sellers sitting in stalls behind their dodgy goods such as AK-47s, M16s, landmines, old uniforms, boots, and helmets. Amputees on crutches hobbled along after foreigners, chasing them down the narrow lanes while holding out a cap and begging for money. Heavy air hung over the claustrophobic interior, where it was easy to get lost among stalls selling pirated CDs or stacked with vegetables or with pots boiling over fires. Old Khmer women squatted beside tables, their mouths a bright red from chewing betel nut, and swatted away flies from hunks of meat.

"You remember those big piles of happy they sold? For five bucks you needed someone to help you carry it."

"Cambodia was in the medical cannabis market before anyone else. They had good reasons in the time after the Khmer Rouge."

"I know, I know. I read Sam's book before you did," said Richard.

We were both already happy, lit up like Christmas trees on Christmas Eve. I ate another piece of pizza, and we paid the bill and headed out to find a tuk-tuk to take us to the book launch. By the time we arrived at the venue, Richard was no longer asking if I felt anything. We walked past a series of long tables covered with elaborate bouquets of flowers. It looked like the wives had cleaned out a couple of flower shops. The expense of one bouquet could have supported an upcountry minor wife for a month. The women circled around the flowers admiring and sighing with approval. A couple of other tables were loaded with finger foods—tiny sandwiches with meat and cheese, and shrimp with red sauce speared with toothpicks.

In the back we spotted another table that was stacked with copies of Sam's book. He was giving them away as gifts to the dignitaries and their wives. If there were high-ranking women officials accompanied by their husbands, I didn't meet them. Sam smiled from ear to ear as he signed books and handed them to the ladies. We watched him from a distance. Richard's smile never left his face, and I was no better. It was as if both our smiles had been surgically implanted. Sam rushed over to greet us. He seemed pleased to find us so happy. He immediately ushered us around, introducing us to officials, none of whose titles or names or faces would lodge in my memory. That's the downside of this kind of happy; it strips your ability to lay down new memories.

There was a raised stage and a TV crew was setting up equipment. Sam left us beside a food table while he walked over to talk to what looked like the person in charge of the TV crew. Richard and I wandered over to an area with chairs and sat down.

"How do you feel, buddy?"

"Numb," I said.

"Me too," he said. "But could you imagine coming to this party without happy?"

Before I could reply, three or four men with their neckties partly undone and the top button of their shirts unbuttoned, wearing uniforms like a ringmaster in a circus, marched past us and headed toward the stage.

"Looks like the band's arrived," I said earnestly.

Richard looked on as the last man filed past where we sat.

"Man, that isn't the band. Those are generals. Some of Sam's friends."

Half an hour later, Sam had corralled Richard and me, one government deputy minister, a couple of generals, and other officials onto the stage. Richard had been right; the men I'd mistaken for the band really were generals. That was pretty much in line with mistaking the woman on the road outside the demining camp for a vegetable seller.

"I ain't gonna speak," said Richard as Sam wound up his speech and looked to his left where we stood. "I can't even remember my own name."

Richard took two steps back, nearly falling off the stage. Sam pushed the microphone into my hands.

I looked out at the TV camera and the crowd. I'd not prepared anything to say. I stood like a silent sentry, holding a microphone. I took a deep breath and started to talk about Sam, how I had come to discover his book, and some of the reasons why the book was important for foreigners to understand what had happened during the Khmer Rouge time in Cambodia. I spoke for what seemed to me like hours, but the actual time elapsed was closer to fifteen minutes. After I handed the microphone back to Sam, the gathered crowd applauded. Richard returned from the back of the stage, saying, "Hey, buddy, that was brilliant. They loved you."

"I don't know what I said."

"Neither do I, but it was beautiful."

The deputy minister came up, handed me his card, and said my speech was the best he'd ever heard. He wanted a copy. I said I didn't have a copy. I wondered if he would remember what I'd said. It didn't really much matter. I'd delivered a speech about Sam and his memoir, and that was what people had told themselves they had come to celebrate. I wanted to say to the deputy minister that he should spend some time at Happy Herb Pizza, and he'd hear a lot of speeches better than the one I'd just given. Sam was happy. Richard was staggeringly happy. I was relieved that some automatic pilot in my brain had kicked in, assembled words into sentences, and sentences into paragraphs that could make sense to a group of people for whom English was a second language.

Once or twice a year ever since, Richard has reminded me of that afternoon at Sam's book launch. Some memories never leave the stage. They re-create past events with ease. Some memories recede into the shadows, out of sight and out of mind, but they never die. What survives is the boiled essence of an experience. Later we fluff the details each time we recall that memory. Whether that is a bug or a benefit of human memory is hard to say; only a non-human memory would be in a position to answer that question.

My memories of the past in Cambodia are tangled up with memories of my past in Thailand, Vietnam, Burma,

New York, Oxford, and Vancouver. Like the entangled particles of quantum theory they communicate over seemingly insurmountable distances and time. What if in the deep future it turns out that the past, present and future are entangled similarly, and through our memory we can shift or influence the flow of time? "Spooky action at a distance" was Einstein's description of the communication between quantum particles. Standing on the stage with a TV camera on me as I pontificated about the killing fields, something from that past found a voice through me. What mattered was I had shared a book of Sam's memories with a group who had vast libraries of much deeper, troubling memories of the killing fields than I as an outsider could have, with content infinitely more profound than I could imagine. I hoped that with the publication of Sam's book, his story might have deepened our understanding of the personal side of Khmer Rouge.

Searching within oneself for buried memories is a bit like detecting landmines. You remember some of the signposts from back then, but the landscape of the present is not the same. It is easy to lose your way when you tunnel backwards in time. My time in the field with the demining team wasn't filed in my brain in isolation. It found a slot on a shelf near the NYPD civilian observer experience. In both cases I was an outsider looking into a subculture that closed ranks when an outsider intruded. Their reaction was to design a river-cruise-like experience tailored to make me feel safe and happy. They'd show me the equivalent of a sunset; they'd serve me up a drink and talk about themselves. I realized this was a piece of theatre and I too had a role to play. But as I had done in Saigon, sneaking into the rafters of the old national assembly, I'd find a position from which to view the unscripted action, to try to discover the telling details that would suggest the real story.

In Bangkok now it is 2017, but in my memory surfing I am in a different time and place; I pull out that volume of Phnom Penh circa 2007 and open it. Inside I discover people, feelings, events, and aspirations that shaped my career as a writer, the choices I made at the time, and the awe that comes from returning to a New York or a Phnom Penh that no longer exists except as memories as fragile as fireflies. I was a member of a small band of expats who experienced those times. Today some of them remember part of what I'm writing about; more importantly they remember many other things that I've either forgotten or never experienced. One worker ant can only leave one scent trail among the hundreds, the thousands, of scent trails others have laid down to the perishable hideaway of mind food.

In the background I've got one eye on the hourglass, the other eye on a constant stream of visions released from my memories of Cambodia. Memories bounce off one another, triggering the release of other memories. A desire most of us share is how we might blow the hatch door to release whole colonies of those mysteriously linked 100 billion neurons.

We divide memory into short-term and long-term. You don't need to have worked most of your adult life as a writer to experience that something a little unusual—something beyond your conscious control—happens to your memory, and as you grow older you find the bright line between the two categories sharpens. I remember Happy Herb Pizza, getting shot at in New York, and jealous deminers' wives far better than I remember who I had lunch with last week or what famous persons died or won celebrated awards in 2009. All of us have to be careful to recognize the lines between marketing, propaganda, and altered mental states, and the actual social interaction that runs through these experiences. Does a fool know that his memories are like fool's gold?

People everywhere are hungry for attention, approval, and funding. That twists what they remember of their experiences, especially if in the cellar of those memories they are haunted by an earlier life of living beside a heap of the dead for four years. If I'd survived the killing fields, the likelihood is great that I would have done to my memories what they did. I'd have buried them, and like the deminers I would have forgotten where I buried them. I'd know there were some people I could share them with and others who wouldn't ever understand the kind of terror people can inflict on one another. I would fill tables with food and flowers and bring in cameras and stand on a stage and say, "Look at me. I'm alive. I survived."

TWENTY-THREE

Here's an invitation to revisit your memory of 2012. Who was celebrated and who died? It's hard to remember the details. For the record, in 2012 the Oscar for Best Picture was awarded to *The Artist*; the Nobel Prize for Literature was given to Mo Yan; the Grammy Award for Album of the Year went to Adele for *21*. Ray Bradbury died that year, the author whose books took us to the stars, and it was also the year that my mentor and friend Barney Rosset died.

By 2012 Cambodia's history of lawlessness, thugs, gangsters, and corrupt politicians had begun to emerge as a source for noir fiction. With my anthology *Phnom Penh Noir* I saw the chance to launch a collective exploration into humanity's history of thuggery through the Cambodian example. Evidence of organized violence has tracked our 12,000-year march to wherever it is we are now, as our species left behind the hunter-gatherer way of existence and turned to agriculture and then industry. The fingerprints of that ancient history of violence are all over Cambodia. The Khmer Rouge took that path to the extreme. Not all thugs are treated equally in the minds of subsequent generations. How could it be otherwise?

The winning thugs write the history books, in which they are portrayed as patriots and heroes; the losers become traitors and common criminals. Pol Pot took a crack at killing all the historians. Just in case any thinker might have seen a job opening for the dead historians, to be on the safe side, he thought, let's kill all people who read books. Let the Old People return to their oral histories. Their truth was always in the tales they told each other. I have no doubt somewhere on earth another true believer will rise to launch another genocide campaign. Cambodia may not be a blueprint for future massacres but it illustrates the irresistible pull of bloodletting among Old People in general, among whom slaughter has always been up close and personal. Their tradition takes no satisfaction in long-distance killing.

In human history it's no secret that many careers and large fortunes have depended on and flourished because of the ability to direct how violence is selectively projected among the masses to instill fear and obedience. The Khmer Rouge were excellent organizers of killing crowds; they knew what drove them to deliver piles of bodies as booty. The Old People had long been under the yoke, and it had cut into their dignity. A large revenge crowd was formed from the usual raw materials of repression, injustice, and powerlessness. The Old People had a long memory of mistreatment and no memory of common cause with the New People. Cambodia was separated into two communities, with a frontier marked by shared bad memories. With *Phnom Penh Noir* I wanted other writers to look into those communities and write about what they found along those invisible frontiers.

Around the world, organized crime cartels have refined the timing and place of violence, elevating it to an art. The Khmer Rouge were a kind of ideological crime cartel for a new priesthood that ritualized murder as a means of cleansing the nation, returning it to purity, and resetting it to Year Zero. The Khmer Rouge merged religion with a crime cartel style of management. They understood from their Paris days that religion was just another system of organized coercion, so they used it as another way to package bloodletting mob organizers. Whether you gut a man based on a utopian idea of society or a religious belief, it sends the same powerful message: we own you.

While I could identify some of the problems raised by Cambodia's recent history, it was more difficult to find writers with the experience, interest, and time to write a short story for an anthology. I began a search for story-tellers, wondering how deep I should look into the crowd of Khmer Rouge supporters for my project?

Thanks to the Internet, many people alive today have seen video showing a steady stream of casualties in one hellhole or another and endless images of bombed-out dwellings, hospitals, schools, factories, and offices. The world is divided between those who have experienced firsthand the effects of such destruction and those who watch it unfold from afar on a computer screen while answering email or leaving a Facebook comment. Very few people remember a news report about a bombing killing dozens or even hundreds in some backwater city they couldn't find on a map. Our memory isn't equipped to process and retain daily instances of long-term violence. That nightly sleep cleans out the news report of yesterday's massacre in Syria. Nor is your memory going to latch on to what comes in the aftermath of organized violence.

When I found my crew of writers, among them were some of the best anywhere, and some of them came to the project with first-hand experience of violence. I'd organized the latest generation of seasoned authors to direct their creative talents to writing about the noir period after the fall of the Khmer Rouge and the Old people were once again out of power. Jorge Luis Borges wrote that "writing is nothing more than a guided dream." Sometimes the dream is a nightmare world that produces the abandoned, unguided dreams of the doomed. The challenge of Cambodia for any observer is to distinguish between the dreamer, the dream, and the nightmare.

TWENTY-FOUR

Violence has always been a profitable industry, and as with other industries, coercive states and corporations have their militarized and civilian sides, dividing up the work and riches generated by violence. It takes a massive amount of support for this to work. War has to be crowdsourced like most ventures. The military blows things up including men, women, and children, and the private sector figures out the best ways to profit from the destruction. As sure as the sun sets over the Tonle Sap River, it also rises over the S-21 prison and a Phnom Penh filled with construction cranes, and the memory of the past is borne on the shoulders of refugees, the injured, and internally displaced landless peasants.

By the time of my initial arrival in Cambodia, that dark side of the Khmer Rouge history, a bridge that lasted four years and connected the mass of country people with Pol Pot and his leadership, was long gone. The mass of Khmer Rouge supporters had disintegrated into individuals dispersed throughout the country. How do justice seekers select the individuals who will pay the price for the mass's genocidal actions? Keep in mind the role of memory in this pursuit; when it comes to individual responsibility, memories differ widely on people's roles. By the time *Phnom Penh Noir* was under preparation, the line between who had fought on one side and who on the other was blurred. When I was with the mine clearing team, I could find little distinction between men who had once been mortal enemies. They were five individuals. I tried in vain to imagine them being part of a crowd seeking out others to kill.

The scale of the bloodletting wasn't something most tourists thought about. "Move along folks, nothing to see here," worked in most places, and in Cambodia that approach became institutionalized as tourists were guided to historical sites where they could walk through carefully curated simulations of what had happened. Aside from attractions such as the killing fields and S-21, most tourists didn't mingle with locals except for the service people encountered in hotels, restaurants, and bars. The poor people they saw were mostly those begging or selling pirated books and CDs on the streets. To these outsiders the poor all looked the same; they were just women, kids, and men hustling them. Foreigners don't much care about who was who or who did what in the past. That past has nothing to do with them.

Even the Cambodians of Phnom Penh weren't certain if these faces from the countryside had had a hand in the killings. It was strange to gather stories for a book in which violence was to be the main theme, when in reality the 2012 Cambodians were working hard to put the Khmer Rouge into a designated page of memory so they could then turn that page and get on with their lives. One might have expected Sam's book launch to be a somber requiem for the countless dead, but it was a lavish social occasion, a party for the survivors. It was as if those who survived had in order to survive emotionally detached themselves from memory of the past. Given what they'd suffered, who could blame them? The lack of memory among the younger generation of Cambodians would soon seal the entrance to the memory vault. When enough people forget, there is no longer any need to wait until the last people who experienced something die. Their memories will already be dead.

The older generation who had directly experienced the Khmer Rouge regime were happy simply to be alive. They still made merit by feeding the monks on their early morning rounds. There were fewer people by then dragging their mangled bodies down the main streets of Phnom Penh and begging for a dollar. The book and postcard sellers were shrinking in number, like the greyhound-skinny kids who ran between restaurants and were shooed away like flies looking to land on a slice of cake. The city had a new sense of energy and hustle. It had woken up, and outsiders with money were piling in to the awakened city. Phnom Penh was back in business. The people wanted their share of the good life. I could feel the same gathering forces of commerce and power that Bangkok had experienced in the late 1980s or early 1990s. Big international aid budgets flowed into government ministries and NGOs, and the money was raked off in all directions. Connected people got rich, as they always do. But there had been so much money in these cases that the spillovers seeded a new middle class.

When you enter the part of Tuol Sleng where the S-21 prison photographs are displayed, you find yourself staring into forgotten lives. Their haunted faces are part of a well-run museum with swept grounds and floors, watched over by uniformed officials. When I'm there and I stop to recall my earlier memories of the S-21 photographs, I have to be honest. The details of the individual faces have faded into a collective memory of an entire wall covered with over a hundred photographs. I wonder if the other visitors will have a better memory of the individual faces than I will. Empathy is supposed to glue these images into our brains.

In my case, on my last visit to Tuol Sleng—and I've been there a number of times—I recognized some of the faces from before, but I also knew that the next week I wouldn't be able to recall any individual one. Our memory for faces is filled with images of relatives, friends, neighbors, colleagues, and celebrities. With billions of strangers occupying the same world, it's not surprising how easily we forget the face of someone we have no connection with other than having once walked on the same planet.

On my last trip to Tuol Sleng, the former school turned into the abattoir called S-21, I stood in front of one group of photos. Most of the inmates the Khmer Rouge had killed in that place were young. Children, as always, were the most vulnerable. They lack even a basic minimum of power to control their own destinies inside a violent adult world. The heart aches when one sees children as victims. My memories drifted into sentimentality until I remembered it was often children killing other children. The simple view that children are good, adults are bad, broke down. We do what we must to mask some of these ugly historical realities.

One thing that had changed since my first visit to S-21 in 1993 was the Internet and social media. YouTube, Twitter, Facebook, and many online media fed the world a steady stream of refugees—on the road, in camps, in boats, running, herded like cattle, and sometimes, dead and heaped in piles. There were always heaps of bodies in the digital world. What the Khmer Rouge had done was edging into the background of history as newer images grabbed the world's attention and memory bandwidth. By 2017 the global bandwidth is now boiling over with information and images. Lost in the vast digital sea, images of S-21's faces bob up and down remotely—if for some reason we remember S-21. Most people don't.

The average age of a Khmer Rouge soldier was fifteen.

That sentence deserves a standalone paragraph. I don't want it lost in a forest of words. The killers and the victims were young. The violence inflicted by an AK-47 round is the same from a child soldier as from an adult. The big difference was financing, training, supply depots, and distribution—those were adult activities. The children followed orders and killed without question.

A *Lord of the Flies* current passed through the cadre in the Khmer Rouge era. What separated vulnerable people wasn't age so much as firepower, discipline, and a few adults with expertise at organizing terror. Cambodia continues to have a youth-dominated population. Around 1993, when I covered UNTAC, the median age in Cambodia was about seventeen. By 2017 it had risen but only to twenty-four. This modern generation was just one cohort beyond those raised in a culture reassembling itself but without teachers, scholars, artists, innovators, and thinkers to lead the way. The Khmer Rouge leadership had tried to blow a chasm into the self-perpetuating economic and cultural system supported by the old regime. That had been the point. The Khmer Rouge genocide was a memory destruction program targeting the cognitive class who processed information and knowledge and passed it on to the next generation. They sought to blow-up the drainpipe where information flowed from the past into the present, lay down a new pipe and restart the flow; it was a historical drainpipe project that almost succeeded.

TWENTY-FIVE

After 1993, with the civil war largely at an end, what was the next step for Cambodia? Government officials had their own ideas. I was more interested in what would happen to the lives of individuals once the armies dispersed. Foreigners living in Phnom Penh arrived for a variety of reasons. The ones I was interested in were of two kinds. First there were the foreigners focused on how best to mend the broken bodies, provide schools and health care, and restore basic infrastructure. Then there were the artistic or creative types who had moved in: writers, poets, singers, musicians, photographers, designers, filmmakers, and performers. The latter group contained foreigners who were partnering with Cambodians to rebuild that other aspect of infrastructure: cultural memory. As I looked around for authors, I doubted I would find anyone who belonged to both groups.

By accident I had previously come across one such person, an Australian who had done work for an NGO and had also started a Cambodian band. Chris Minko, a classically trained musician from Melbourne, had worn both hats. For many years Chris ran an NGO that provided support for landmine victims. He found international resources to fund the purchase of artificial legs. He also organized a wheelchair basketball team that won tournaments, and those victories delivered a sense of pride and dignity to a group of people who'd been robbed of both. He'd been living in poverty raising a daughter as a single parent. Living on street market food in a Phnom Penh slum, he had made the kind of difference most people will never achieve, but after years the work, the lack of money, the red tape, and the bullshit had worn him down. Like a nail that had been pounded down and yanked out one too many times, he found it hard to go back to the construction site. But with this experience he had an ear to the ground inside communities most foreigners didn't know existed.

There is more than one way to make a difference in the lives of others. Ask people anywhere if making another person's life better is important, and most of them will tell you it is. We think of our family and friends. A handful of people expand their range of generosity and empathy to include outliers and the estranged—two categories of people we normally don't think about as having anything in common. An outlier is someone who intellectually, socially or culturally attitudes sets them apart from most people in society. The estranged fit the psychological profile of someone alienated or disaffected. In Phnom Penh the reality was that the underclasses drew heavily from both powerless groups. Chris Minko wrote songs about their lives.

Chris had contacted me in Bangkok around 2010. He asked if he might use some phrases I'd written in *A Killing Smile* for a song he'd been working on. I told him to go ahead. He later wrote "The Ying," drawing inspiration from the lyrics of my novel. Chris had read the book when it had come out in 1991. When *A Killing Smile* was published in Bangkok, it became a local sensation for a couple of months. The front window of Asia Books on Sukhumvit Road displayed copies. I walked into a Villa Market a day after a book review appeared in the papers, and every other shopping cart had a copy stuck between the bacon and milk.

The novel, set in the basement of the old Thermae, a massage parlor and seedy after-hours "coffee shop"—wink, wink, nod, nod—on Sukhumvit Road, had caught on for a couple of reasons. As Jack Reynolds's *A Woman of Bangkok*, published in 1956, had showed, there was an audience for a novel set in the Bangkok underworld. Much had changed in the city since then. No subculture remains stable over time, and that was true of the world of Thai prostitutes. Like all subculture hangouts, the Thermae had its own insider language, style, values, and shared expectations.

Tourism in Thailand really opened up in 1988, designated Visit Thailand Year. That was Thailand's foreigner Year Zero as planeloads of Western men arrived and a number of them fell in love with a girl they'd met in a bar, the Grace Hotel, or the Thermae. Like Mao's little red book, the original red cover of *A Killing Smile* was popping up everywhere for a while. Chris had been in a relationship with a woman from that world. She had later died from a drug overdose. Almost twenty years after that "The Ying" was released, its lyrics presenting a jagged shard of his memory of a woman and a relationship he couldn't save from self-destruction.

During late 2011 and into 2012, I recruited authors, organized and edited their stories for *Phnom Penh Noir*. The noir style had become popular among international crime fiction readers. No one had yet done a collection of stories set in Cambodia. In a market with noir titles ranging from *Pittsburg Noir* to *San Diego Noir*, there was no doubt that an anthology set in the shadow of the killing fields could find a readership in Europe, North America, and Australia.

My association with Sam Sotha's memoir of the time of the killing fields led me to believe that there were many other witnesses, faceless and voiceless, with untold stories and there was value in recording those stories. But there was an ever present danger in seeking out such stories. Reconciling with the past meant setting up a memory exchange and expanding those memories to a larger, modern audience through stories. In the world of noir no clear line divides good from bad; institutions are tainted and corrupt, officers of the state brutal and ruthless. Cambodia didn't have to audition for the noir role. It had lived noir. At the same time I understood that no book—no library of books—could ever contain all that had happened during the years of terror and misery. But *Phnom Penh Noir* was an attempt to create a collaborative memory project.

Roland Joffe, who had directed the Oscar-winning movie *The Killing Fields*, released in 1984, was a veteran at capturing the noir of the time. His film had done more to dramatize the era than perhaps any other single artistic work. After the film was finished, Roland maintained ties with Cambodia, funding a number of charitable projects, including Chris's NGO. I had other connections with Roland from the past. One of my neighbors in New York City, Spalding Gray, had a leading role in the film. I didn't know Spalding well, but he and I had a couple of conversations about his time in Cambodia during the shooting of the movie. The "memory" bug had bitten Spalding there. When he returned to New York, he wrote, produced, and starred in the one-man performance film *Swimming to Cambodia*. Roland and I also shared the memory of another Hollywood personality. Stirling Silliphant, who'd won an Oscar for his adaptation of *In the Heat of the Night*, had been my close friend until his death in 1996. Roland had known Stirling from the time when both of them were on the Hollywood party circuit.

I approached Roland about contributing a story to the anthology. Not surprisingly, he tried to beg off, saying that he'd never written a short story before. Once the magic dust of an Oscar touches you, the next thing that happens is you are on the receiving end of a constant stream of offers from producers, publishers, actors, agents, writers, and total strangers asking for something. It's impossible to keep up with the correspondence and still have a life. Most famous people simply ignore inquiries like mine. Silence is golden. But my connection with Chris Minko made that more difficult. Also, Roland had a continued interest in the people of Cambodia. I promised to work with him on the story, and that finally sealed the deal and he signed on to the project.

Roland set his short story inside the NGO world of high ambition and low greed. "Hearts and Minds" which drove a silver stake through the heart of the shameful, corrupt side of the charity-funding business, exposing the metastasis of fraud and advantage-taking in Cambodia. James Grady, whose novel was turned into the Sydney Pollack film *Three Days of the Condor*, and John Burdett, who established himself with the detective novel *Bangkok 8*, also brought star power to the anthology. It was a lesson Stirling had taught me: no matter how good your script, without star power you'll open in two backwater cinemas in Kansas. To get attention for an anthology, it helps if you have authors with a track record of focusing millions of eyeballs on a book or film. I was fortunate to have scored a hat trick with Roland, James, and John.

With my high-powered cast of foreign writers in place, the next mission was to talent-scout Cambodian artists, and writers in particular. I started my search like one of those mine clearance teams, not knowing quite where to look but having a vague idea. My early search also brought home to me what the country had lost. Its intellectual class was still rebounding, and most of the educated new generation thought their creativity was better served by going into business and networking. After what their parents had been through, did they want to voluntarily struggle to make a living with a paintbrush or a word processor and keyboard? The Cambodian attitude was recognizably the modern human attitude. I found lots of people who had endured hardship, humiliation, and danger, and all they wanted now was the full redemption offered by the consumer society. There was no looking over the shoulder at the jungle they'd escaped. But there was another reality: if anyone did return to the past to examine what had caused things to fly about, it was the artists and authors.

Through some detective work I found Bopha Phorn, a young investigative journalist who worked for one of the English-language newspapers, the *Cambodian Times*. She had written a powerful story about pedophiles, drawing on her investigative experience gained from covering an actual case as well as the trial of a foreigner charged with a sexual relationship with a child. Another contributor, Kosal Khiev, a Cambodian born in a Thai refugee camp, had left as a kid for America and landed in an American prison when he was sixteen. Eventually the Americans had deported him to a home he'd never known, where he used the only skill he'd learned in prison, rap poetry, to turn a fire hose of hurt and anger on the broken society he found in Cambodia. I'll return to his story in a later chapter. Suong Mak, a young gay writer, was the only locally published author among the Cambodians represented in the book. For all of these local writers the anthology was a chance to be noticed by an international reading audience. Chris Minko and his Cambodian lead singers brought the noir beat to the rhythm post-Khmer Rouge life of Phnom Penh.

TWENTY-SIX

When I comb through my memory of Phnom Penh in 2012, I remember a series of meetings attending to the problems of organizing and participating in a string of events. Notable among these meetings were talks with Roland Joffe to raise money for charities and business discussions with the Foreign Correspondents' Club Cambodia, the venue where we launched *Phnom Penh Noir*. At Sam's book launch five years earlier, I'd only had to talk into a microphone for a quarter of an hour; someone else had done all the work. Assembling artistic, business, and political people into a co-operative group isn't easy anywhere, and it wasn't easy in this case. But once the book launch had happened, a more important problem came into view. The launch was a successful party for the 250 guests who attended, but had anyone not on the guest list taken notice of the book?

Phnom Penh Noir was launched into the world, and the sun continued to rise and set over the Tonle Sap. Nothing substantial shifted in the careers of those who contributed to the volume. Dozens of other noir anthologies have subsequently been published. As the world has become a much more noir place in the half decade since, *Phnom Penh Noir* is looking like just another brick in the noir wall. When I reread the book recently I found that most of its contributions have held up well as stories. But the reality is that, ordinarily, stories change very little in the lives of their readers. Who among them will remember any story in the long term? The odds for this volume having an impact are low and getting lower as people's memory batteries devoted to noir approach exhaustion. As culture consumers we may become supercharged to look for that new book, image, or article, but the book, image, or article of a week ago already belongs to the past and is mostly forgotten. Five years ago seems like another lifetime. We struggle on the information treadmill, feeling its pace pick up, overcome by the growing awareness that our attention can't process the necessary volume and speed. We fall behind. We feel the beginnings of despair. But we can never give in to those feelings.

Two quotations from George Orwell had driven me forward on *Phnom Penh Noir.* "The best books," he wrote, "… are those that tell you what you know already." And the other quote: "Writing a book is a horrible, exhausting struggle, like a long bout with some painful illness. One would never undertake such a thing if one were not driven on by some demon whom one can neither resist nor understand."

To tell us what we already know is to revive our memory of what we know. Some historical events require our artistic workers to create public reminders of their existence, or else the awareness of madness and evil will fade from collective memory.

My memories are separated into small time locks like those in a canal. Traveling down a canal with locks requires co-ordination. Each lock is a chamber where the water level can be lowered or raised, with the boat falling or rising with the level. Something similar operates in our brain structure, allowing us to navigate memory, and forces outside us have done a great amount of tampering—let's call it whitewashing—so that what we remember is only vaguely connected with what actually happened. Our memories based on life-defining turns in our lives or emotionally charged moments have the best chance of surviving the purging of synapses as we sleep. The evolution of memory is one that favors remembering violence. We read about people being killed. We see clips on the TV and online— these are the canal locks where the whitewashing occurs. It's hard to assess how much the whitewashing has scrubbed away the truth. Few people have actually witnessed the body of a murder victim or been shot at, or walked through a minefield or war zone, or had a gun pointed at them. I can check off three of the above.

Even if everyone had experienced three out of four violent scenarios and lost none of the detail, retaining these memories in perfect clarity, we couldn't necessarily pick out the whitewashed details. Our experience is limited to what we saw from our physical position in the scene, and that is a narrow perspective from which to draw conclusions. Someone ten meters on the other side would remember something different. Once you pull back from these examples and take into account that much greater levels of violence have gone on for millennia, you can see that part of that history is the reality that such knowledge has done almost nothing to vest us with an appropriate sense of humility about the scope and power of human memory.

Earlier I mentioned that the average age of a Khmer Rouge soldier was fifteen, but I left out the larger history of child soldiers. The river of history has many chambers filled with child warriors. Some historical sources tell us that the Children's Crusade of thirteenth-century Europe swept up an army of 30,000 children. They were assembled to kill Muslims. Nine hundred years later, floating inside our own historical chamber, we remain at war with the Muslims.

What historical details of the Children's Crusade can we examine to help us on our river journey? The answer is we don't have many. The basic challenges of navigating downstream through memory can be found in vagueness of the history of the Children's Crusade. What happened, who these children were, what kinds of weapons they carried, the logistical problems of food, sanitation, shelter, and organization, and other details are lost inside the deep hole of mythology and fable, our time-honored memory-manufacturing machines. Is the figure of 30,000 children reliable? Who knows? But our memory banks love these nice, round figures; they are easy to remember, and we tend to assume what is easy to remember must be true.

As story-tellers we are drawn to narratives that unfold specific lives. Those stories once provided the glue that bonded members of a community together. In modern times the technique has been adopted to promote patriotism and nationalism. A competing type of story, based on data, is told within modern communities bonded by impersonal statistics, which tell abstract stories where the individuals disappear inside large numbers.

Our memories are selective. We remember stories longer than we recall statistics, though intellectually we may accept that statistical data are more reliable in measuring and predicting future outcomes. Few people can switch off the personal story-telling channel and tune in to the abstract, rational, statistical analysis of data. Our wiring prepares us for stories based on experience, and even when they are worthy guideposts as we navigate our way through the world, our memories of them don't remain stable over time.

We suffer from the habit of pulling our memory files from only the most available drawers. I draw far too much from what I saw, heard, or read yesterday. What happened in Cambodia's past, as in most countries, is eclipsed by a protective halo of lies, half-truths, cherry-picking, assisted forgetfulness (whitewashing), and dissembling. As I looked into Cambodia's obscure past I realized I'd seen this kind of halo before. In the early 1980s I'd written two radio dramas about the relocation camps where Japanese Canadians were interned during and after World War II. The Canadian camps were not extermination camps, but as examples of racism, injustice, and mass hysteria, they stand out in North American history. *The Bamboo Pillar* was broadcast on the CBC and *View from Cambie Bridge* was picked up by NHK, with an introduction recorded at NHK studios in Tokyo read by me. With these projects I had started writing about historical violence, detention camps, and the madness that infects the reasoning of an entire society.

My Canadian experience in researching a number of Japanese Canadians who had spent time in the camps may explain, in part, my interest in the Khmer Rouge forced-labor camps. That background of state officials removing people from their homes and lives and housing them in guarded camps was a thread I wanted to pursue in *Phnom Penh Noir*, and that's why I sought out stories—personal stories—of survivors of the killing fields.

"Reunion," my own contribution to *Phnom Penh Noir*, revolved around a convenient lie that became the basis of the personal myth of one Khmer Rouge boy soldier. Sam, the main character in the story, has founded his adult identity on one untrue story, a powerful one that everyone has accepted as true. The fact that no one has questioned Sam about his lie has made each repetition of it easier. The lie, polished over decades, has rewarded him with speaking engagements, dinner invitations, and employment opportunities. Sam's lie, like the best of creative stories, achieves authenticity from its small, telling details; it also casts Sam, the young narrator, as a hero and showcases the casual evil of the adult world of violence. We are suckers for such elaborate lie-tellers as they confirm our deepest suspicions about human nature: our species is ruled by the most inhuman, senseless, primitive, brutal, violent men among us.

TWENTY-SEVEN

In 1975, the year of the Khmer Rouge takeover in Cambodia, one of life's little ironies was reflected in the awarding of the Oscar for the Best Picture to *The Godfather, Part II*; the Nobel Prize for Literature was won by the Italian poet Eugenio Montale; and the Grammy Award for Album of the Year was given to Stevie Wonder's *Fulfillingness' First Finale*. Both Jimmy Hoffa and Francisco Franco died that year.

In the dominance game, raw brainpower and knowledge matter little; it is the ruthless, decisive use of force that separates the winners from the losers. You might be smart, but rational arguments rarely defeat someone who has the license to shoot you dead. History records the winners' version of the story of violence, justifying murder as part of a noble narrative of heroes, loyalty, bravery, and glory. That's the story the Khmer Rouge told each other when they had power. Why should they have been any different from the murderers who preceded them? A weapon pointed at someone is a powerful incentive for that person to forget that the weapon bearer's story is a lie. People learn to survive by forgetting murdered victims. The living accept the gunman's version of history and move on with their lives. By the time I entered Cambodia, the Khmer Rouge, in an important respect, had ceased to exist. But though a political and military structure may be defeated, for its followers and supporters, in significant ways, what has driven them to murder hasn't vanished. Their memories of the time they had the absolute power of life and death are largely kept to themselves. If you dig into the past where the memories are hidden, you might stumble upon an abandoned map drafted by forgotten ghosts describing a different psychological landscape. Official memory maps are the ones we turn to when following paths into the past. That's why it is easy to slip and fall down the side of a mountain of lies.

The birth and death dates of Democratic Kampuchea, the military dictatorship of the Khmer Rouge, are 1975 and 1979. Those dates appear clean, firm, and exact. In 2017 they invite us to believe that all of the cruelty, nastiness, and evil of that time expired almost forty years ago and can be left to historians to sort out. In reality, those dates are part of the great illusion of the passage of time and its relationship to the events of man. We continue to feel the effects of the French Revolution, an event that ended over two centuries ago; those ideas and the consequent killings and institutional upheaval continue to work their way through modern times. We can be easily persuaded by the reasons governments provide to justify actions against perceived enemies. We willfully are blinded to the real reasons behind the massive stockpile bombs and guns. In earlier times the inventory of weapons were different—crossbows, knives, swords, or spears but the motivation remains the same. Those with the best, most powerful and advanced weapons win the competition for best story—the story of why it is necessary to exile, imprison, "disappear," or kill people, to create structures to support the killing process, and to provide immunity to the killers.

The fall of Rome is a good example of the centuries that can pass before an old order, old ideas, and old institutions run out of steam. Contemporaries didn't live long enough to witness how everything fell apart. It was a slow process that required attention to details to see. It's not as if some large void opened, swallowing the intellectual, moral, emotional, and spiritual lives of the survivors. What happens at such times is a slow winding down of cultures, societies, and civic and governing institutions.

The Roman emperor Romulus Augustus was captured and sent into exile by the Germanic leader Odoacer in 476 CE. Romulus was the last Roman emperor in Western Europe, and his overthrow has become the accepted date to mark the fall of Rome. The period that followed was called the Dark Ages. On the landmark date of 476 CE it was unlikely anyone thought Rome had fallen. That realization occurred over the centuries after the fall. There were no Nobel prizes, Oscars, or Grammys then to use as milestones. We have adopted new reference points to mark and remember the passage of time. Awards and prizes, which are frozen moments of time, have become features of our shared memory palace. But unchanged since the Roman days is the fact that the consequences of regime change and societal collapse ripple through systems for long periods of time. What does it really mean that the Khmer Rouge regime fell in 1979, when the meaning of their fall from power continues to echo through the present?

We have faith that our memory benefits from centuries of data and analysis, and that includes the era of the fall of Rome. Over the following several centuries, it became clear at some point that the candlelight of memory had been blown out. That age might also be called the Great Forgetting. When a civilization collapses, it unleashes a farrago of cultural, social, economic, and political unravelings. Memory of the past shrinks to a burnt ash from that fire. Knowledge of that civilization's agriculture, science, arts, engineering, and so on disappears. When this happened in Cambodia in the Khmer Rouge years, the nation's prior institutions, culture, and knowledge networks collapsed into a localized dark age of forgetting.

Cambodia's equivalent of 476 CE came on 17 April 1975, when the Khmer Rouge marched into Phnom Penh and established the Communist Party of Kampuchea as the governing entity. Pol Pot was Cambodia's Odoacer, whose violence had put an end to a previous regime. In 2017 only forty-two years had passed since the Khmer Rouge takeover. That would have corresponded to 518 CE in the former Roman Empire. Romans would have just started to experience the effects of the Dark Age, but centuries would have still passed as the evidence of the loss accumulated: collapsed bridges and aqueducts, a plunge in agricultural production, the disappearance of metallurgy and construction techniques, and the like, as prior knowledge was lost. Roman civilization had lasted for five centuries. The Khmer Rouge lasted only a tiny fraction of that time. While Pol Pot's regime existed in the blink of an eye compared with Rome, the forces responsible for creating the Khmer Rouge didn't suddenly disappear in 1979, nor did the people. You can find some of them today in riverside slums, among the landless living upcountry, and in the alleyways and slums of Phnom Penh.

What sets the 1975 to 1979 period apart is the sheer scale of the slaughter. Most of us can't quite wrap our minds around the numbers. In a four-year reign of terror the estimated number of killed, starved to death, or dead from disease was in the range of 1.7 to 3 million. Only a few of those faces stare out at today's visitors to S-21. Multiply those faces until you reach 1.7 to 3 million and consider the size of the wall you'd need to display their photographs. It's estimated that between twenty-one and thirty percent of all Cambodians perished. In the past century only the World War II Holocaust and the Holodomor or Ukrainian genocide from 1932 to 1933 exceed the raw number of people murdered. Try to imagine what millions of dead bodies would look like if stacked in neat rows. What you would see before you would be, not heaps of dead, but mountains of them. Most people would look away from such a sight. But artists and writers won't allow us to look away; that's one of the essential functions of art—to commit to collective memory such horrors, as Picasso accomplished with his painting *Guernica.*

In 1979, the year when the Khmer Rouge were forced out of power, Nazi death angel Josef Mengele died, as did Nelson Rockefeller; the Oscar for Best Film was awarded for *The Deer Hunter*, a bleak Vietnam War movie; the Grammy for Album of the Year 1979 was awarded for *Saturday Night Fever*; and the Nobel Prize for Literature was awarded to Greek poet Odysseus Elytis.

In the modern period, our legacy of mass murder has been recorded in films, books, paintings, photographs, and poetry. What I'd requested from the authors of *Phnom Penh Noir* was to ask themselves two questions: How does an artist or writer archive the memory of the survivors, as well as those who perished, in an era of mass murder, and create a meaningful legacy to their memory? A complete representation was impossible, and any partial representation was bound to be faulted for its inadequacy in measuring the suffering. But obstacles like those shouldn't stop us from making and using maps. *Phnom Penh Noir* is a small map. My approach at the time was to ask the authors to write about the effects of the genocide's aftermath on those who survived and their children and grandchildren. At least in this way we had a chance to dramatize the baggage that the living were carrying with them into the future. Exploring the content in those individual bags meant exploring memories.

Looking back now at the world of 2012, five years ago, it is difficult to imagine that I possessed this degree of optimism about what authors or artists could contribute to the remembrance legacy. I believed it was important that future generations shouldn't forget what we are capable of doing to one another. I wasn't alone in searching for answers about the lives uprooted and destroyed by the Khmer Rouge. A substantial series of documentary films has helped preserve the experiences of Cambodians in that period and since. One of the earliest was *Cambodia: Between War and Peace*, shot in 1991. Later documentaries include *The Land of Wandering Souls* (2002); *S-21: The Khmer Rouge Killing Machine* (2003); *Enemies of the People* (2009); *Red Wedding* (2012); *The Missing Picture* (2013); and *Storm Makers* (2014). From forced labor camps to forced marriages, to the systematic executions of an entire class of Cambodians, these filmmakers have left evidence of multiple attempts to record into historical memory the impact of the Khmer Rouge. Jorge Luis Borges wrote in *The Book of Sand & Shakespeare's Memory*, "We forget that we are all dead men conversing with dead men." In Cambodia those dead men conversations are inscribed on tombstones that we call books, film, poetry or songs.

TWENTY-EIGHT

Five years after *Phnom Penh Noir* I've found myself floating down the river of hope without a paddle and in a leaky canoe, watching as the history of the Khmer Rouge recedes while comparable forces threaten to overtake other countries. From my position on the river, the collapse of Cambodia into a genocidal state is looking more and more like an omen from the past that the modern world hasn't fully deciphered.

All the books and films about Cambodia were a crash course to prepare us for our time. When the Cambodian cards are laid down once and for all, who will it be who has interpreted their meaning? Today we have the same cards again: the Fool, the Magician, the High Priestess. The same options stream through our memories like the faces of a deck of Tarot cards, and when we read them, we read what others wish us to read. We absorb into semantic memory a narrative that has been massaged and doctored, and we believe not only that it's true but that it's our own memory.

In the future, if this memory manifesto is revisited, an AI many times smarter than any human being may assess our memory capacity, distribution, and input and output systems, and it won't be difficult for it to spot the many problems inherent in human memory. We thought our history was a record of the war between good and evil, right and wrong, and reality and illusion, when in fact it was a hack loaded into our memory and accepted as our own creation. What we fail to appreciate is that we don't experience reality through our memories; we re-enact experiences. Memory is only a re-enactment, but subjectively we perceive it as what actually happened.

The wiring of our brain can't be undone. In our memory re-enactments we suffer from "buffer overflow" caused by a surfeit of information. That's why we grab on to what is most available, plausible, and simple, assuming that those bare-bone qualifications make it true. In reality we have little choice. If the full information floodgates were left open, the operating system would crash. The Dark Ages were an operating system crash. The Khmer Rouge years are another example of a memory system overload and crash.

History is littered with such crashes. In our time, the existential threat identified by many scientists is that an AI of vastly superior intelligence could exponentially magnify and project accustomed degrees of violence against humanity, and as a result humans would live under the boot of machines. We have reasons for this fear of domination and helplessness. A casual look at history can reveal how each technological reboot has been used to scale up the amount of violence and to expand the space where it could be projected. For the Aztecs Hernán Cortés and his Spanish conquistadors were their existential moment; the Aztec civilization was destroyed by a technologically advanced small group of men who subdued them with the speed and skill of a killer AI. For good reason we nurse a fear that we are the new Aztec Empire and the AI ship has been sighted approaching the harbor.

Most of us are preoccupied with making a living, watching a movie, attending a sports contest, spending time with friends and families, and saving for our children's education.

Memory Manifesto

The dial on our memory is more likely set to remember a parent–teacher meeting on Thursday rather than it is to recall the lessons of history, science, and mathematics. We find it difficult to drink from this fire hose of information, but we've lost the will to plug it. We pay a cost for that uninterrupted access. In the last American election, at the end of 2016, the buffer crashed and Donald Trump ascended as the man to refill the collective memory. Trump has promised a journey back upriver, where those living on the banks will once again be in control of their own destiny. No such communities exist or ever existed. That hardly matters. Pol Pot showed that reality can be made irrelevant to what matters if you embrace the old culture and mythology. We seem never to learn that it is religion and ideology that have created the killing fields of the past, and they will do the same in the future. We've forgotten the reality of the past and are in re-enactment mode, drawing on borrowed memories and building a false edifice with the bricks of angry dreams.

Jorge Luis Borges wrote "Paradise will be a kind of library" To which I would add a footnote, "Hell will be a place where all libraries contain books filled exclusively with lies."

TWENTY-NINE

Writers, photographers, filmmakers, and painters share the same creative dilemma: what historical perspective can they bring to the contemporary context that makes their art a bridge between the past and the present? What part of the big, messy story do you wish others to pay attention to? The light of the past strikes a prism at different angles, producing different possibilities. Out of multiple choices, what compels an artist to select one angle over another? By definition, any scene, event, or personality that is excluded becomes a political statement.

Cambodia's history challenges the creativity, talent, and originality of artists addressing it. The pursuit of fresh, new perspectives requires a dedication to the observation of people, incidents, landscapes, rivers, boats, schools, prisons, and hospitals to discover what the rest of us have failed to see as we walked past. These perspectives require patience in a rushed world. I'm in a hurry like the White Rabbit with the pocket watch in *Alice's Adventures in Wonderland*, running laps inside my terminal of memory, flitting from the present to the past to the future. "I'm late! For a very important date!" That line from the Disney version of *Alice* could be our society's epitaph. We hurtle forward as we speed through the hall of mirrors that our memory works, in a fashion that ensures we will always be late in our appointment with the truth.

We are forever racing against time and memory re-enactments. Scientists speak of space-time—one word. There is a case to be made that it is actually space-time-memory, again written as a single word. Some believe that the universe is a mathematical object, that it is information. If that is the case, memory is the way information processes and replicates itself through time and space. From the beginning of our species, our memory has expanded and grown in depth and volume, and that has transformed who we've become.

I stumbled upon an alley in Phnom Penh that served as a time chamber. The alley was near Peter Klashorst's walkup garret. One afternoon, peeking through his laundry hung like a curtain on the balcony, I spotted it. Between the painter's shirts and pants I saw the entrance to a narrow alley located halfway between the Lux and Larry's Bar on Street 136. Our memories of stories shape our identity and sense of self and place. The alley pointed me like a compass to a connection that exists between story-telling and an unexplored place in time.

Place defines us, provides us with a sense of identity or alienation. Place has an emotional effect in many ways. Think of where you are from and how that central place in your memory colors the way you see it and the way you see other places, too. Our sense of identity comes from our connection to a place. We divide the world between, on the one hand, where we were born and raised, where we've lived since, and where our family and friends live, and on the other hand, the places we've merely visited or read about. Foreign spaces have, at best, a weak pull on our memory and an even weaker pull on our sense of self and the allegiances and loyalties associated with "our" place. We don't have a worldview of place; it remains local and specific in our minds. The existence of so many unexplored places should remind us that we don't really have a worldview of place. We are confined within our local view of the canal; we stay a lifetime inside one lock, with the past locks stretching behind us and future ones disappearing into the horizon before us.

If you find the right spot, though, you can use hitch a ride down the river of space-time-memory. The world has many such spaces like that alley of Street 136. We pass them but they don't attract our attention. Those are, for me, the best places to find stories. Places lost in space and time can be filled with memories no one has bothered to collect. If an author can unearth those memories among the people occupying that space and connect them in time to a reader, he or she has given the reader a new and powerful navigational guide through a chamber of space-time-memory.

I like the idea of how the Polynesians in ancient times found a way to read the night sky like a book. For their seafarers, the stars told stories. The stories they told could be shared with others, who passed them on, perhaps sung to music, until those stories became part of the collective memory of the Polynesian people. Once sailors could recall from memory the stories in the sky, they could know their place and set a direction. The night sky, seen as a memory map, allowed Polynesians to successfully spread through thousands of miles of the Pacific Ocean. The Polynesians were the ones who discovered that stories could be reliably used to define place and time. Meanwhile, the Greeks hugged their coastline.

I remember the names of some of the constellations—Orion, Pegasus, Taurus, and Boötes—all of them because of stories. The early Polynesian story-tellers had guided human memory to create our own literature from starlight. The old tradition, it seems, was for story-tellers to look to nature; they recorded the stories nature told through objects in the sky, rivers, and thunderstorms. These were the stories that allowed for long-distance seafaring and that in turn allowed exploration, long-distance trade, and new wealth. Stories about nature became stories about gods, and those stories evolved into stories science told. Scientific stories were a new kind of story-telling in which the magic and enchantment were boiled away, leaving only the material facts.

We live in an age when a vast number of the stories humans have told each other have been lost or are incompletely remembered. Our written stories extend back across the last six thousand years. And on Street 136 I stood at the entrance of an alley thinking of Polynesian sailors' eyes uplifted to the night sky. We can't look at patterns in the sky or in an alley without turning them into a story.

On 17 April 1975 the Khmer Rouge declared Year Zero. The Pol Pot regime reset the Orwellian clock of history. The Khmer Rouge forcefully removed over a million people from Phnom Penh—no one has any precise count as the city had filled up with refugees—between 17 and 23 April, after which Pol Pot entered a city emptied of its inhabitants. Schools, banks, government offices, businesses, shops, pagodas, and hospitals were all stripped of people. The story of violence in this case wasn't a classic photograph of piles of rotting bodies; this story was a city devoid of life. It seemed likely to me that people had cowered in the alley I saw before me. They'd been dragged out, beaten, and marched out onto Street 136 on their way to the killing fields.

I thought of Polynesians looking at an empty sky and trying to find meaning somewhere. It's hard to tell stories about emptiness. We naturally seek to escape the void. It's through our story-telling that we've remained hopeful that if we look hard enough, we can discover in the empty space some elementary particle that can be a signpost.

In 2017 Phnom Penh bustled with a slurry of people as thick as Cambodian fish soup—tourists, tuk-tuk drivers, beggars, small shop owners, officials, and market stall vendors. The street lights had been switched on. I entered the alley off Street 136 and it was as if I'd discovered a small piece of 17 April 1975 curled up in another space-time dimension.

I'd had a reason for keeping my eyes peeled for a scene that spoke volumes over time. Peter Friedrich, my long-time German translator, and I had decided to collaborate in bringing out a new edition of *Zero Hour in Phnom Penh*. It was a Calvino novel, the third in the series. White Lotus had originally published it as *Cut Out* in 1994. Unionsverlag, a German-language press located in Zurich, had published a German edition under the title of *Zero Hour in Phnom Penh* (in German, *Stunde Null in Phnom Penh*) in 2003. The book had been translated into a number of languages and had even won a couple of literary prizes along the way. The German language rights had recently returned to me from Unionsverlag, and Peter and I had set out to chart a new course for the book on our own. Like a couple of Polynesian sailors in a dugout in the open sea, we hoped for the best.

For reasons of German copyright law and practice, the title was changed to *Rendezvous in Phnom Penh*. If the names of the constellations had been changed as often as the title of that book, even the best seamen could be confused. Cities, populations, and book titles are like piles of sand with each new grain added until at the critical point of disequilibrium the whole thing collapses. I'd returned to Cambodia to find a scene that would provide a powerful visual story about the place for the new edition's cover.

The alley around the corner from Peter's studio was such a place. I photographed people going in and out of the alley one day, and the next day, I found the same alley empty of life, a place for a destitute person to sleep. The photographs were a study of a self-contained universe that shifted moment by moment, that was never stable or still. I thought what Jorge Luis Borges wrote about "a Talmudic legend about three men who go in search of God. One became insane, the other died, and the third met himself." In Cambodia the legend needed editing. One went crazy. The second one's skull was displayed on a shelf at S-21. And the third curled up in an alleyway and dreamt he was lost in labyrinth with no center.

Phnom Penh Alley 136 Street Phnom Penh 2017

This was as close to an empty Phnom Penh as one could find in 2017. Not a whisper of life. Was this a glimpse into the past of Phnom Penh, a ghostly image reminding me of what being devoid of human beings meant inside a city? The meaning of a story is inevitably drawn from the perspective of the story-teller. If we flip the same alley on its side, it takes a moment or two to get one's bearings. What is it? It was Leonard Cohen who taught us that a crack is how the light gets in. Reading the light among the machines is reading stories into stars. Humanity has a long history of finding stories in those cracks of light and stringing them together into powerful stories.

Woman in Phnom Penh Alley 136 Street Phnom Penh 2017

The visual effect shifts once a young, smartly dressed woman is caught in mid-step, like a fly in amber, walking down the alley and carrying her lunch. The story of the alley depends on movement or the absence of life. The perspective is dynamic, and no one shot can be said to be the story of the alley. What a writer brings to the task is matching the place with a story about that place. Substitute for the pretty young woman a rumpled, sleeping man, and the alley is transformed into a seedy, squalid place. The possibilities of danger, crime, and dissolution require more than just an empty alley.

Man sleeping in Phnom Penh Alley 136 Street Phnom Penh 2017

There was no single story of that alley. There were many different stories to choose from, and that is an intrinsic problem of story-telling: as one story surfaces, the others recede from view. Whenever we think of a place, it is with a story attached; it is an identification technique that allows us to store the place in our memory in a way that we can't store time. In a real, tangible way, we possess a built-in pre-Copernican belief system that locates my place as the center of the universe. To think that the place that is the source of my identity is no different from any other place, and is not in any way favored over other places, remains to this day a bitter pill that we still have trouble swallowing.

When the time came to choose the cover artwork for *Rendezvous in Phnom Penh*, it wasn't destined to be a scene from the alley off Street 136. I'd failed to create anything like a navigation guide with the alley pictures. As much as I tried, I felt readers would pass the alley by, just like the vast majority of people who walked down Street 136. I needed a different story. Like the Polynesians the sea draws me in inexpressible ways that solid land cannot. To get my bearings and pass them on to readers, I needed a storyboard in the sky. One star. Our star. I wanted passengers to follow me to a place, the Phnom Penh of my past, of my imagination and memory. A fireball of nuclear fusion teaches us about our place in nature.

The Tonle Sap River had seen many sunsets since 17 April 1975 and will see many more. It is strange how our imagination, drawn from our memory, fuses what we remember, what we've heard, dreamt, seen, and felt, like hydrogen converted into helium in the process that we see as sunlight. This is the process that turns on our inner light. Like the sun, our imagination burns until it exhausts itself. People and civilizations die just like stars that run out of fuel. We are of a period of duration. That's why we frantically seek a place to stand and from which to look out, a vantage point that helps us understand our place in the universe.

In 2000 I sat with Barney Rosset at an outside bar in Patpong, near the entrance to the Star of Love. I'd been listening to Barney, in between fresh orders of rum and coke, tell stories about Henry Miller and the legal battles he'd fought on behalf of Grove Press over obscenity charges against *Tropic of Capricorn*. Barney never tired of talking about Henry.

I asked him, "What if Henry Miller hadn't gone to Paris but instead had gone to Bangkok? Would that have changed things for Miller?"

Barney looked at me with a big smile.

"It would have changed everything.

197

That is the gravitational pull of a place and time. It changes who and what stick in your memory. A place makes you who you are and hitches your life to a star, one that you follow for a lifetime. Once you are in tune with the networks of the place, the scent trails you've laid down run deep into your memory. Without your being aware, a place molds you by the choices it provides, and the choices you make become the subject of your life.

Toule Sap, Phnom Penh 2017

THIRTY

I remember being in front of a dimly lit Phnom Penh bar, walking between the outside tables where customers sat. I was trying to decide where to park myself for an hour before meeting Peter Klashorst for dinner. I went inside the bar and sat on one of the stools. I watched the manager and a server, both women, at work behind the bar, carefully rolling impressively large, tightly packed joints. The server would show the manager each of her creations and the manager would nod. The finished product would be added to a small pile. From the way the manager's hands moved, I could imagine she advertised herself as an expert, like one of those cigar rollers in Cuba who had turned a mundane skill into an art. The server played the role of the apprentice who showed promise.

A middle-aged foreigner with thinning hair, dressed in a polo shirt and jeans, sat three stools down the bar from me. He'd ordered the joints. He sounded lonely and needy, and was trying to engage the apprentice in conversation as she worked. She finished rolling a joint and held it up, admiring her work. In front of the foreigner a dead joint end, crushed to a pulp in an ashtray, rested beside his beer. The evening had a quiet, languid feel. Two- or three-word utterances prevented the conversation from falling into complete silence. Rolling joints had given the staff something to do that was more satisfying than speaking broken English with the customers.

It was seven-thirty or eight on a weeknight. None of the people at the bar looked like they worked for a living. Not that they looked wealthy; on the contrary, they looked unemployable. I wandered outside and sat at one of the tables. Outside the bar a different story was being told. Three Africans stretched their long legs at a table in front. They'd saved money by buying beer at a local store down the road. A server came out to chase them away, but they wouldn't leave. Then the manager came out and unplugged the fan that was cooling them as they drank.

"Why you do that?" asked one of them.

"Fan cost money. You no pay money, no fan."

"It's hot," said one of the African men.

"Buy a beer and I'll turn it on."

They stared at her, glassy-eyed, sipping their beer from convenience market plastic bags. The great migration had brought people there from around the world. On Street 136 you could find many of them washed up with little or no money. Half an hour later, one of the Africans left to buy a couple of more beers from a nearby shop and then returned to share them around the table like trophies. The three men looked broke but not broken—sullen but not hostile, relaxed but alert to those passing along the street. The Cambodians, like the Thais, had an informal social hierarchy of attractiveness based on skin color. At the bottom of the totem pole was black skin, deemed ugly, repulsive, bad, dangerous, and dirty. Stationed at the top of the heap, white skin was beautiful, wholesome, good, inviting, clean, and safe. Your worth and acceptability were judged by the color of your skin. The skin color of Africans matched the ebony black found on a deep, infinite night, through which their eyes and teeth shone like moons and stars.

None of the bar staff volunteered for the job of throwing out the Africans sitting with their outside beer. The Africans showed a pack attitude that made their intention clear: nothing short of physical violence was going to move them from this watering hole. Like Maori warriors performing the haka, they used their faces and bodies to communicate the terrorizing force that comes from total unity on the battlefield. So far the conflict had been a series of indecisive skirmishes. They didn't look like trouble so much as just extremely large and immovable. The Cambodians who came out looked tiny by comparison; they just stared at the Africans before retreating back into the bar. It looked like the kind of ritual that would end either in one side giving up its ground or in violence.

When you live abroad, you learn to sense when people around you are signaling a problem. Places like the bar I'd stumbled onto are owned, and that comes with the right to exclude others, but property law isn't that simple when it comes to squatting at Street 136 tables in Phnom Penh. I put my bet on the Africans holding their ground for as long as they wished. They gave every appearance of liking the table, the view, and the surroundings. If only they could have a fan turned on, they'd be the happiest non-customers the bar had entertained in a long time. I had a choice of space to make. I could hang around outside and find out the Africans' stories, or return inside with the potheads and witness how cannabis plays chords on the memory of the user.

In musical terms memory plays out like an orderly Philip Glass composition for some and the unanchored creative flight of Keith Jarrett's *Köln Concert* for others. Music and memory are closely linked. In the nineteenth century, when Cambodia was a French colony, Mussorgsky composed *Pictures at an Exhibition* as his way to honor the memory of his artist friend Viktor Hartmann. The painter had died suddenly at thirty-nine from a brain aneurysm. Art has the power to preserve the memory of an artist who likely would otherwise have been forgotten. In this case Mussorgsky's composition showed the power of music to fix a series of paintings into long-term collective memory.

We remember paintings, faces, places, and events we have experienced, but we cannot take in the full reality of the world into our memory. Most things inevitably get left out. In art, every artist or writer feels the agony of making those choices. In life, most of the time the choice is made without our knowing it. Only fools believe completeness is possible. We suspend disbelief as a result. We have to in order to image the complete body in motion through time and space from a piece of shin bone.

Back inside the bar, I pulled out a stool next to a young foreigner who was just an inch or two under seven feet tall. He was with a Cambodian man. The young man sipped on a beer while the Cambodian stood at the bar without a drink. The African squatters still sat outside, and a bona fide giant sat at the bar inside. I hoped that I'd made the right choice.

The conversation in the bar had picked up, and a buzz of dreamy voices circulated in the small room. The smokers had relaxed, shedding some of the weight of the world they normally carried on their shoulders.

I imagined how Richard Diran would have characterized the bar—as Happy Herb's Pizza with happy but without the pizza. Come to think of it, I'd never seen an African at Happy Herb Pizza or adjacent restaurants. Street 136 attracted the low end of economic refugees who endlessly hustled tourists, the girls, and one another. Inside the bar, a better-off class of refugees drank beer and smoked, humming to themselves and breaking into their own memory vaults to loot the contents. A gray cloud of smoke hung over the bar as the customers puffed away, talking in the big-hearted stoners' mode of early evening.

The giant sitting on my right was an ex-American professional basketball player. He was in his mid-twenties, dressed in smart clothes, and homesick. He told me his story. He'd been recruited to play basketball in Asia, where the sport had a growing number of fans. The basketball players who were cut from the NBA might not have survived the competition of NBA play but still had the skill and world-class moves to run circles around the local players in Asia. Of course, they also towered over them like construction cranes over a riverside slum. Next to the basketball player, the Cambodian man in a suit and tie and—get this—a vest under the suit hovered like a nervous coach on the sidelines during a timeout. I'd seen his type before: part thug, part gofer, part bullshit artist. They were a dime a dozen in all big cities. In Phnom Penh you could buy a couple of dozen for less than a dime. I pegged him as a wannabe tough guy who lived under the shadow of the powerful and fed on the scraps thrown to him. He leaned over the bar counter, breaking into the conversation each time the basketball player paused.

"My people will take care of it," he said. "I know places no one else does in Phnom Penh." A wink, a nod and a sinister grin. "No one can touch you when you're with me," he said, smiling as he toyed with his cellphone.

He was the mouthy type who bragged about his connections, money, and women. The action started when he grabbed the bar manager's arm. His move was ambiguous. While it appeared playful, there is a hint of violence in any physical touching of a stranger. When a physical space is violated, it's impossible to know what will happen next. The move caught her by surprise.

The Cambodian suit said, "Where is my smoke? I ordered it before that guy down there." He pointed at the middle-aged foreigner at the end of the bar who sucked on a freshly rolled joint. "I ordered one before the foreigner. Why you ignore me?" he asked with a rising anger in his tone.

"I tell you before, you not buy a drink, you not smoke in my bar." She twisted out of his grip. "What you want to drink?"

"I don't want a drink," he said. "I ordered a special cigarette."

"This is my bar. You don't order me."

"I don't want a drink."

"Then no smoke. That's the bar rule."

Her reference to rules seemed odd in what was clearly a fairly lawless establishment—non-customers squatting at an outside table, joints being rolled behind the bar, a Cambodian quasi-tough guy demanding a special smoke. I'd fallen into a sinkhole where the rules were fluid.

"Do you know who I am?"

That was the classic response in a time and place where connections to authority carried more weight than the law.

"I don't care who you are or who you know."

He picked up his cellphone and dialed.

"I'm phoning the prime minister's office," he said, pointing his cellphone at her like a gun.

The manager was in her early to mid-forties. She folded her bare arms, leaned forward, eyes bulging.

"Phone him. Tell him you are in a classy bar on Street 136 and this woman won't roll you a smoke. "

The tough guy was about her age. They'd been raised in the same Cambodia, knew the same language but chose English as their verbal weapon to wage a personal conflict.

"My army people will be here in twenty minutes to close you down."

"And the prime minister will send the army?"

"He will close you down."

I was glad to have chosen not to stay outside with the Africans. The action was inside between the Cambodians.

"Fuck you! Get out of my bar!" the manager said. "Now!"

The basketball player had long since stopped talking. He sat with stooped shoulders, looking abandoned and sad in a way I imagined he looked the day he was cut from his NBA squad and sent to the showers for the last time. The stoners in the bar were lost in smoky conversations about women and nightclubs.

"You can't throw me out," the suit said.

"I am ordering you out. Get the fuck out of my bar! And don't come back."

A thick silence filled the air. Conversations at the bar stopped. Outside, the Africans continued to chatter among themselves, unaware of the menace growing inside.

I pay attention to precursors to violence. Evolution has prepared all of us to be on guard when a predator shows its fangs. You then have a choice: back down or move forward and engage. Status, face, dignity, and power are at stake. What happens next is a big unknown. How you move and when you move are split-second decisions that come from your culture, temperament, upbringing, and genes. Some people are wired for violence; most are born pacifists. That largely explains the history of violence in which psychopaths rule over the rest of us because we don't want to get hurt.

The tough guy froze for a moment. He had a choice to make as he dialed someone on his cellphone. No one was picking up the phone at the other end. He put the phone on the bar counter. It crossed my mind that he might be packing a gun in a shoulder or ankle holster. Cambodia, like Thailand, had a gun culture as crazy and unpredictable as America's. And if he did, I wondered, would he pull it out? I'd lived in Thailand's face culture long enough to know that when a man loses face, he loses any sense of rationality, and he might storm out only to storm back in a half hour later with murder on his mind. In thirty years of living in Thailand, I'd never seen a Thai woman throw a man who claimed high-level connections out of a bar. It was inconceivable.

The basketball player slid off the bar stool and stood upright like a giraffe ready to pick leaves off a tall tree.

"Let's go," he said, paying for his drinks.

The tough guy had been given his excuse, his way of saving face.

"Only if you want to."

"I want to," the basketball player said.

If I could have given him a Most Valuable Player award on the spot, I would have done so.

"I'm still phoning the prime minister's office," the tough guy said to the bar manager.

"Tell him he's welcome anytime. But he has to buy a drink. Just like anyone else. And if he could do something about the Africans outside, tell him I'd be grateful."

Now that he was heading for the door, she was fucking with his pride.

The two of them, gangster-hustler and basketball player—mismatched in size, age, ethnicity, and personality—walked across the length of the bar and out the door. That was a long walk of shame for the Cambodian. None of the customers at the bar paused their drinking or smoking as the two passed, except for one guy who said in an Aussie accent, "Mate, you ought to play basketball." He wasn't talking to the tough guy. The basketball player smiled, shook his head, and said, "That's what my father said. Thanks." They disappeared past the table of Africans and filtered into the crowd on Street 136.

I'd been given a small lesson on dealing with volatile, potentially violent situations. The manager could have got into a fight with the Africans who'd refused to leave and complained when the outside fan was switched off. But she'd let it go. She let them be. The rule of no outside beer wasn't strictly enforced, but it wasn't exactly waived, either. She might have even felt sorry for them; they were so ragged, dirt poor, and downtrodden, maybe she didn't have the heart to press them to leave. But when it came to another Cambodian, someone roughly her own age, with the same set of memories of the past, who was throwing his weight around as if he were a big shot, well, that was a different kettle of boiled fish. She would take a stand. It was a glimpse of the reason why civil wars are more bloody, brutal, and protracted than wars between countries. Brother against sister, brother against brother, cousin against cousin... and soon no one's house is safe. Pol Pot had a kind of genius for getting relatives to slit each other's throats.

A place like the bar I found on Street 136, with its vivid emotional geography, lends itself well to the role of memory palace. All you have to do is mentally place what you wish to remember somewhere within the scene, from the outside table to the bar counter to the shelves behind the bar. Put all the facts and numbers you want to retain in specific places. Later, when you wish to remember, mentally call up each part of the scene and find the artifact you placed there.

At the end of the bar I placed the memory of an old friend's Academy Award. Stirling Silliphant had won an Oscar in 1967 for his adapted screenplay for the *In the Heat of the Night*. It was about racial relations in the old American South, and at the end of the story a bigoted white sheriff carries the bag of a black man at the rail station. When I want to remember that divides can be healed and our tendency to scapegoat and reach for a gun can be overcome, I think about the end of the bar and remember a tough guy who stood down in the face of a determined woman who'd called his bluff. He had neither reached for a gun nor carried anyone's bag, but he had walked away. Walking away is good enough.

Carrying your enemy's bag as a show of respect only happens in the movies. It's one of those Oscar-winning moments that we wish could happen in real life. We wish it represented how bigoted people's behavior can change with experience. But fifty years after Stirling won his Oscar, in the actual world people would no longer believe the sheriff might carry the black man's bag.

THIRTY-ONE

I've heard people use many excuses to cancel a meeting, a class, or an appointment. But one such excuse stands out amid my memories of Cambodia. In 2012 I traveled back and forth between Bangkok and Phnom Penh four times. On the second trip that year, on 25 April 2012, thirty-seven years after Pol Pot had entered an empty city, I had an appointment to meet a Cambodian writer, Bopha Phorn. She had sent me her draft of "Dark Truths" for *Phnom Penh Noir*. I'd planned to go through my line edit of her draft with her. We scheduled to meet on 27 April 2012. The night before, Bopha phoned to cancel our meeting. She explained that she'd been upcountry working on an assignment for her newspaper when something had happened—she didn't offer any details—that prevented her from returning to Phnom Penh. I'd never spoken to her before, so I didn't have a baseline from which to interpret the emotion in her voice, but she sounded anxious, tired, and scared.

"Is something wrong?" I asked her.

After a long pause she said, "It's not safe for me in Phnom Penh."

She seemed overly dramatic. It was my turn to pause.

"Why wouldn't it be safe? Are you in some kind of trouble?"

"I'm staying with a friend for a week or so. You should come upcountry. It's beautiful in the country. We could go over my story."

"It would be better if you came to Phnom Penh," I replied.

I had other meetings and obligations. It wasn't possible to drop everything to go upcountry to meet an author for an hour or two.

"It's quiet here," she said.

She went silent again.

"You sound afraid," I said.

"We have never met. How can you tell if I am afraid?"

"What I can't figure out is why you won't come to Phnom Penh. You live and work here. And what I'm hearing is that staying upcountry is safer? I have a feeling you're not telling me the whole story."

"No place is safe," she said.

"Okay, but what are you doing upcountry?"

I thought a neutral question might draw her out.

"Investigating a story for my newspaper."

"And did you get the story?"

"I saw a soldier shoot Chut Wutty."

"You saw someone shot?"

"Yes."

"Where were you when this happened?"

"I was sitting next to him in the front seat of a car. After he was shot, the soldier pointed his rifle at me. An officer told him to put down his rifle. 'Don't shoot the girl,' he said."

Those four words had likely saved Bopha's life. Having got the reason why she was afraid to come to Phnom Penh out of her system, she gradually explained her situation. It was my turn to feel fear, not my own but her genuine fear. I was having one of those phone conversations that you never forget. How many times do you talk to someone who's gone into hiding after witnessing a killing by someone immune to the forces of the law?

Later I learned the background of what had happened that day when Wutty's vehicle had been stopped and he'd been killed, as the basic facts filtered out. Chut Wutty, forty years old, an environmental activist who founded and acted as director of the Natural Resource Protection Group, had been shot dead by a member of the military police. Wutty started a campaign against illegal logging. He had gathered evidence of who was behind the harvesting of resources from national parks. He'd driven two journalists, Bopha Phorn and Olesia Plokhii, on an investigative trip that had included taking pictures of the illegal logging sites. The line between military police and military soldiers was a thin one upcountry. A lot of environmental damage was being done, and those who had a financial interest in extracting resources didn't like Wutty's activities or the exposure he was bringing to their illegal business. He'd become a pain in the ass—which is the one thing you want to avoid in Southeast Asia if you want to see your next birthday.

Some people are born with courage, though they are rare outside the movies. Others, who might be considered the truly courageous, may be shaking in their boots, but some inner voice tells them they are doing the right thing, making a difference, healing the earth, and protecting people. During the UNTAC period in 1992–93, Wutty had been an electrician's helper for the Canadian contingency. He was someone I might have passed during the time I reported on UNTAC. He'd have been about six years old at the time Pol Pot and his Khmer Rouge remnants were chased to the countryside along the Thai border. He'd grown up in the rough and tumble post-Khmer Rouge period. The day his life ended violently, he'd been driving by a checkpoint manned by soldiers at Veal Bei Point in the Mondo Siema district of Koh Kong Province, located in the southwestern part of Cambodia.

Bopha had seen a man killed next to her. This wasn't a TV drama with actors and fake blood. She'd been plunged into a real life-extinguishing incident, with all the blood and pain and fear that accompanies a violent death. She had then seen the military policeman pointing his rifle at her, his soldier's finger on the trigger. She was next in the line of fire. Only a last-second intervention had saved her and the other journalist in the car, a Ukrainian woman.

Most writers have to hunt down stories; for others the stories hunt and haunt them. Nothing prepares anyone for the critical moment when violence explodes. Bopha knew that she was lucky to be alive. For a few seconds that had stretched to eternity, she had been next in line for execution. The swift sequence of events had left her giddy.

Like every act of violence, every intervention to stop such an act has its repercussions. In Bopha's case minutes passed amid confusion, chaos, and shouting, with doors opened and people dragged out. All the time the witnesses feared that someone higher-ranking than the officer on the ground might see things a different way and order a different outcome. Bopha and Olesia had witnessed Wutty's murder. The two live witnesses weren't country peasants and couldn't easily be intimidated into silence.

A death like Wutty's could normally be explained as an accident or a suicide. But with two live witnesses to the shooting, the usual lies would be a difficult sell to the international community. The soldiers knew that ultimately the ones who would need convincing would be senior members of the military and political players, a group who would not wish to risk sanctions and funding cutoffs.

Donors from around the world had poured massive amounts of funding into Cambodia with the purpose of lifting it out of its killing habit. The idea that Pol Pot–style executions of activists were still happening upcountry was an awkward, inconvenient fact. It made outsiders ask if their assistance and aid was all for nothing and wonder whether the killing fields had ever stopped. It seemed that rather than exterminating all the intellectuals, activists, opinion-makers, and thinkers, it was sufficient to kill only the most troublesome ones as a warning to the rest that if they crossed a line, they too had no protection.

Conveniently for some, the military policeman who shot Chut Wutty, a thirty-one-year-old named Rattana, died at the scene. The press reported that Rattana had been hit by a ricocheted AK-47 round from his own weapon. For practical purposes, that ended the matter. There was a perfunctory investigation afterwards, but the killing was quietly allowed to disappear from public view.

At the time Bopha spoke to me on the phone, it wasn't clear how things would turn out and whether Bopha remained at risk as a material witness to a killing. After the shooting Bopha had gone to a hideout. She wouldn't tell me over the phone exactly where she was staying. Her call to me was one of the first she made after Wutty was shot. She'd also talked with her family and her colleagues at her newspaper. The shock of what she'd witnessed hadn't worn off, and like anyone in her situation she was terrified that the powerful men who were behind the illegal logging would consider her a liability.

"You'll be safer in Phnom Penh," I said. "I can't help you upcountry, but I can help you here."

"How can you help me? You're a foreigner."

One of my rules of engagement with another person, especially one who is at risk, is not to over-promise what

I can do. Playing knight in shining armor or bodyguard can be a vanity that gets people killed. I knew that I was very close to overstepping that line. She was right; I was an outsider there, and as much as we outsiders liked to think we had influence, in reality we had close to none. Physical safety is paramount in such cases, but feeling safe is also a state of mind. Once people enter the state in which no place feels safe, it's difficult to reach them. If she could trust me, perhaps I could help. I told her I would make a phone call.

"Who can you call?" she asked.

That was a legitimate question, and her skeptical tone let me know that I likely had no idea how things worked in Cambodia. Of course she was right, but I also understood that sometimes all you need to do is to stretch out the time line. Each day that passes between such an event and the present makes the witness safer than the day before.

"I can get through to the Prime Minister's office," I said. I was careful to frame what I could actually do.

"You know Hun Sen?"

"No, I don't. But I have a friend who does. I'll call him."

"You'll do that?"

"I'll do it tonight."

I knew a lot of people in Phnom Penh, but there was one person I trusted who had the right connection to power. Chris Minko, who'd become widely known for his work in the humanitarian community, had received a medal from Hun Sen. Chris had a direct line of communication with the Prime Minister's office.

For anyone who might be perceived as a troublemaker in a country like Cambodia, Thailand, Vietnam, or Burma, the first order of business is to shelter under the umbrella of a powerful figure. The governments in these places operate like glorified protection rackets, looking after their cronies, relatives, and business associates. But they are savvy enough to know that protecting someone outside that group can be an opportunity to look good to other people they need to do business with. It could also give them the upper hand when dealing with upcountry warlords. Sometimes power is the delicate balance of forces of violence. It was likely that the company behind the illegal logging in Koh Kong Province had their own high-ranking officials in the military and the government covering their backs. It was a given that everyone involved would have been on the phone to powerful backers, letting them know a shit storm had been stirred up and they needed protection.

The essential point was that the military would be implicated in the illegal logging upcountry that had cost Wutty his life. It was unclear whether my efforts would protect Bopha or would only complicate her ability to survive. Years of living in Southeast Asia had taught me several lessons. For instance, I knew that what was important wasn't anything that might be said to Hun Sen but the mere fact of the call to his office. The word of that call would get out to those who needed to know that his office had been contacted and they'd better not make a bad situation worse. Most of the time that sort of action was good enough. I couldn't be sure in this case, though, and if I was wrong, then it was possible that my involvement would put Bopha's life at additional risk.

I remembered my experience with the NYPD and how rapid-fire decisions led to actions that one would have to live with afterwards. I believe the military policeman who shot Wutty must have made just such a split-second decision, only he didn't live long enough to regret it. I'd also learned in Thailand that if a person can stay alive for forty-eight hours after witnessing something the authorities wish to suppress, the odds of his or her survival are greatly increased. At that point a targeted killing will likely be seen as counterproductive.

When I revisit my memory of 2012, I can hear myself talking to Bopha on the phone about my connection to the Prime Minister. In retrospect I am embarrassed at what a clichéd and shallow piece of comfort I'd given. On the other hand it was all I had to offer. On the surface there wasn't much difference between my little power play and that of the diminutive Cambodian hoodlum who wouldn't buy a drink at a Street 136 bar and threatened the manager with his big-league political connection. He'd been playing offense, and I'd been playing defense, but essentially we were playing the same minor-league game. In terms of height, he didn't reach the NBA basketball player's waist, but in the world of political power, that was an irrelevant point. In this neck of the woods a small man with big connections would beat a tall man every time. The small man who stood on the shoulders of power could simply drop the ball through the hoop and block all the big man's shots. Like it or not, that was how the game was rigged. In basketball terms, I didn't even come to the knee of the powerful men who ran Cambodia. But I resolved to bounce the ball of luck and take a shot at the basket from my corner.

After the call from Bopha ended, I phoned Chris Minko and explained the problem. He promised to make some inquiries. As Bopha turned up in Phnom Penh the following day, it may have been that those inquiries had worked to send a message that Bopha had someone inside the system asking about her welfare. That is the kind of inside information someone like me on the outside could never access. The answer was scattered over time through many different sets of memories. Sometimes making a phone call works. Sometimes the message is passed to the wrong person or not passed along at all. Foreigners, no matter how good they believe their connections to be, are likely to fall short; they simply possess less power over the players who are running the inside game than players' cronies, school chums, relatives, and business associates. Foreigners come long after that queue has filed through the door of power. It's their court, their ball, their rules.

Trying to pick up the trail of causation runs cold once you enter the world of dense, opaque political and commercial networks. The deep feudal network works like the old Cold War of mutually assured destruction, or MAD, when each side understood that firing a nuclear missile would cause its own annihilation. The Cold War warriors hadn't invented the MAD policy out of whole cloth; MAD was an old policy adapted from corrupt tyrants and feudal lords in their dealings with their underlings. Each minor corrupt official had dirt on others in the chain of command and control, giving the official a dirt pile to be used in case of an emergency, but because the official had his own dirt to worry about, the weapon rarely got used.

All I know is that Bopha felt safe enough to return to Phnom Penh the next day, though not safe enough to return to her own home there. She arranged to stay with a friend. We had lunch at the Java Café, one of those upscale expat restaurants with a California-style menu. She arrived a bit before me and sat at a balcony table. I spotted her immediately—a young woman in her twenties, fragile, petite, with large glasses on the end of her nose as she read the menu. Forty-eight hours earlier the man sitting next to her in a car had been shot dead.

She looked up and saw me. We'd never met. But the telephone conversation we'd had while she was upcountry had established a bond.

"Thank you so much for helping me," she said.

"I didn't do anything," I said.

I wasn't being humble. The fact was I hadn't done anything other than make a couple of phone calls to Chris Minko.

"I wouldn't have come back unless I believed what you said was true."

Not every noir anthology editor has a conversation with an author trapped in a personal noir drama more compelling than any story found in his book. To me it seemed anticlimactic to talk about her literary story after the real events she'd just been through, but she couldn't wait to get down to work.

"Did you like my story?"

She looked at the envelope on the table. I'd brought along her manuscript, thinking she could go through the changes later.

"I made a few comments and suggested some edits," I said.

"Can I see what you wrote?"

I slipped her story out of the envelope. I'd placed little yellow sticky tabs where I'd made changes or edits. The manuscript had a massive number of the tabs. I saw her smile vanish at once. She looked up and I saw a sense of dread as she composed what she wanted to say.

"Was it that bad?"

Nothing any editor says about a story can rise to the level of badness that comes from witnessing someone next to you getting shot to death, but most writers fear disapproval. The verdict of "bad" attached to a piece of writing strikes the author with the same emotional chords as standing on a scaffold while an executioner, humming to himself, slips a noose around one's neck.

"I liked it," I said.

That made her relax.

I wasn't in the mood to talk about the story that she'd written. I wanted to hear the details of her experience upcountry.

"Can we talk about it?" she asked.

"What happened with Wutty?"

"I want to talk about my story, if that is okay."

I saw that the yellow tabs I'd attached to the pages had drawn her attention.

"An old friend named Stirling Silliphant taught me how to use tabs. He was a famous Hollywood screenwriter. The first time he had lunch with Norman Jewison, the director of *In the Heat of the Night*, Jewison put Stirling's script on the table. He told Stirling he loved it. Stirling didn't see the love. He saw his script buried in a confetti of yellow stickers, leaving only small patches of white showing. Jewison and Silliphant had many lunches afterwards, and each time Jewison would tell Stirling he had done a wonderful job rewriting the story while presenting the latest manuscript version still covered with tabs, though fewer in number. These lunches continued for some time. At their last lunch only one yellow tab remained in the script. Stirling felt vindicated at last."

"What was the last comment?"

"It was about the train station scene. A redneck sheriff played by Rod Steiger carries a black lawyer's suitcase. The lawyer was played by Sidney Poitier."

"Why didn't he carry his own bag?"

"He could have done. The writer was making a point without using words. In a film you can do something an author can't do as well on paper. Who carries a bag tells us a lot. As a show of respect, the sheriff lets the lawyer know that he's accepted the black lawyer as an equal."

"That scene wouldn't happen in Cambodia," she said.

She was right. In Cambodia, in an upcountry town, one of Rod Steiger's men would have shot Sidney Poitier dead. Roll the credits. That would have been the end of Sidney. And it would have been the end of Sidney's desire for a better world. Hollywood endings are different; they twist the events of the actual world and invent a fairer world we want to believe we live in. In the real world the railway station scene with the bag, that last yellow tab on Stirling's screenplay, was a fiction, planting a false memory with mass audience appeal. Outside the cinema, in the bright light of day, people did no such thing. If you were happy to incorporate a fake memory of the civil rights movement into your worldview, no one would stop you, and there would be plenty of people who shared the same fake memory to form a community.

As a rule of thumb, Cambodia teaches a different lesson: don't confuse a counterfeit memory with a genuine one. If you make that mistake, you run the risk of ending up like the environmentalist who was gunned down because he believed in the kind of ending from *In the Heat of the Night*. The thought of carrying a meddling outsider's bag, especially one who'd come to town filled with a burning desire to bring justice, equality, and fairness, was inconceivable.

THIRTY-TWO

Under the Khmer Rouge a generation of Cambodians had suffered an immense number of casualties. Thousands more who'd escaped the killing fields had fled the country by foot, cart, or boat with just the shirts on their backs. The mass tide of Cambodian refugees had a role to play in the memory puzzle. It was a twenty-year problem.

In the period before the Khmer Rouge takeover of Phnom Penh in April 1975, fighting had been going on for years in the countryside. The city absorbed a mass exodus of rural refugees who hoped to escape the war. My friend Luciano Prantera had gone with a South African friend to Phnom Penh in 1972. They'd flown into the capital in a four-engine plane filled with pigs, chickens, produce, and large sacks of rice. Phnom Penh was then under siege. Their plane circled the airport in a holding pattern while two planes of Lon Nol's vastly diminished air force took turns dropping one bomb at a time on Khmer Rouge positions on the city's outskirts. After each bombing run, the plane would return to the airfield. The other plane would take off while the returning plane loaded another bomb. The bombing runs lasted about half an hour as Luciano and his friend watched from the window of their airplane circling the airfield. It was a crazy place to visit in 1972. It was like flying into Aleppo in 2016 out of curiosity about the country and its people.

A few days after Luciano and his friend landed in Phnom Penh, they hired a motorcycle and drove out of the city. A couple of boy soldiers with AK-47s waved them down, pointing at the road ahead. The soldiers were in the midst of a firefight. They advised Luciano and his friend to turn around and go back to Phnom Penh. When the incoming rounds started from a position a hundred meters ahead, they decided to call it a day and drove back to the city.

A few days later they travelled on to Vietnam, which also was in the midst of war. They heard from a friend in Phnom Penh that the same plane they'd taken from Bangkok to Phnom Penh had been shot down; it had crashed and there had been no survivors. They'd flown into a city that had run low on food and supplies. Old-fashioned sieges were effective in the Middle Ages and were still an effective military strategy for the Khmer Rouge in 1972.

In the Khmer Rouge years many ethnic Vietnamese were killed, and survivors fled by the thousands to Vietnam. From 1979 to 1981, after the Vietnamese chased the Khmer Rouge out of Phnom Penh into remote areas, around 630,000 Cambodians fled through minefields and war zones to seek refuge in camps along the Thai side of the shared border. About 150,000 children under age fifteen awaited relocation to other countries.

I have no personal memory of the refugee camps strung like a broken necklace along the Thai-Cambodian border. My wife, Busakorn Suriyasarn, worked for two years at Phanatnikhom Camp, a processing center for refugees waiting for resettlement, located in Chon Buri Province. Freshly graduated from Chiang Mai University in the late 1980s, she taught refugees how to use a Western style toilet, keeping a checkbook, supermarket shopping, among other cultural elements of life valued by and expected of people living in the West. Her two years working as a counselor at a refugee-processing center have since occupied a special place in her memory. She once told me with firm conviction about her refugee camp experiences, "Those were the best years of my life." That remark became for us one of those standing in-jokes that husbands and wives share, but I do believe those years were the best for many who worked in the camps. The reality was the refugees taught her lessons in human dignity and resilience. Her refugee memories have mixed with my own memories of the period into a collage that is common between husband and wife.

Over the years I've heard stories from friends who worked in those camps—John Fengler, Steve Rothstein, and Rob Burrows—that suggest my wife was not alone in this feeling. That leaves an astonishing irony. One group's best years coincided with the worst years of another group, whose lives had a very different set of memories. A memory DMZ ran between those who had a choice to work to help others find a new life and those who had no choice and saw the camps as interim prisons from which escape was difficult.

As is often said about such experiences, you had to be there to understand it. If you don't have a direct experience of a particular time and place, you are left to process the second-hand memories of others. You can find all the facts and details of refugee camps you like, but you can't download the feelings and emotions that come from living and working in such a place.

During the time of these mass migrations in Southeast Asia, the Americans had a different attitude toward refugees, one of acceptance—sadly, that attitude is less prevalent today. In a gesture straight out of *In the Heat of the Night*, in the aftermath of the Khmer Rouge rule, the American government accepted 136,000 Cambodian refugees within its borders. France accepted 32,000 refugees, and the Canadians and Australians accepted 13,000 each. These Buddhist survivors of a civil war had been given a chance for a new life. But the refugee-accepting foreign nations also bore much responsibility for what had happened, dating back as far as the 1789 French revolution, which was an inspiration to Pol Pot, and of course the Khmer Rouge were aided and assisted by the massive American secret bombings of the country as an extension of their Vietnam War. Much of the opportunity the Khmer Rouge saw for imposing a radical social reset came from abroad.

Over a thirty-year period I've discussed life in the refugee camps with NGOs, journalists, and UN officials who'd worked at the Khao-I-Dang camp near Aranyaprathet in Prachin Buri Province, Thailand. The Thai military ran the camp, and it was the only place the Thai government recognized the legal status of the inhabitants as refugees. But not all camp residents were so lucky. Even the camps were geographically in Thailand, there was evidence that Khmer Rouge "controlled" five out of eight refugee camps. The bitter division within Cambodian society was reflected in the leadership of the camps. In some camps the noir hell of the Khmer Rouge metastasis had found a new location to sow its ideological seeds.

THIRTY-THREE

One of my goals for *Phnom Penh Noir* was to find someone who had been processed as a refugee through one of the refugee camps to share his or her story. I found a young man who'd been born in 1980 in one of the camps in Thailand. Rake thin, heavily tattooed, with a tense, guarded smile, Kosal Khiev was culturally more American than Thai. Over coffee in Phnom Penh he told me his story of immigrating to America as a child along with members of his family, including three brothers and three sisters. Kosal had adjustment problems in America. His new life was difficult, his surroundings alien. His only friends were street gang members, and their friendship was the only one offered. He joined a gang at thirteen, and three years later, after a shootout that left two other people seriously injured, he was processed again—this time by the American justice system. Kosal spent the next fourteen years in prison. Upon his release the Americans deported him to Cambodia—a country he had never known. He arrived in Phnom Penh a stranger, penniless, with no friends or contacts. He slept rough for a few months.

While in prison he'd had a casual conversation with a black inmate who encouraged him to join a class that taught writing, specifically rap poetry. For someone who had made his bones on the hardscrabble inner-city streets of America, poetry at first seemed as far away as Cambodia. It was an abstraction. Kosal took a chance and attended one of the poetry classes. Soon he was hooked. He devoted his years in prison to perfecting a rapper's poetic voice. By the time he was released, his anger, heartache, and disillusionment had found a channel of expression. For the first time he found a source of pride in his life that wasn't based on violence. Intense, motivated, and talented, he soon became a minor celebrity in the fashionable watering holes of Phnom Penh for his unique rapper lyrics. It wasn't long before others outside Cambodia began to notice this small, heavily tattooed diamond in the rough who'd served a long sentence for attempted murder.

The irony wasn't lost on anyone that Kosal had served more prison time than any of the Khmer Rouge leaders who had organized the genocide. Kosal and Bopha both witnessed the chimerical darkness buried in the souls of ruthless people. They understood in the way we can't comprehend except in the abstract—that power is capable of inflicting widespread damage. Some were able to rise above the dislocation and violence. They didn't let their personal experiences define them as helpless victims. One lapidary phrase they both would agree with is "Life ain't fair. Get over it." Better yet, turn the pain into art. They both made that turn into the world of creativity.

The BBC invited Kosal to talk about his life. He did a powerful TED talk where he rapped about his experiences. The TED producers had asked him for a script months before his appearance. They asked again weeks before and again days before, until finally he told them that he wouldn't know what he'd rap until the camera was turned on. They'd simply have to take a chance on him. Otherwise, no deal. It was the same for the story he did for *Phnom Penh Noir*. He didn't write it. He rapped the lyrics to "Broken Chains," which I recorded and had transcribed. Here's a sample:

> Let me beak it down. I'm breaking down. Pound per pound. Break dance you around to the sound of broken chains. It's broken rage. Home broken set to the stage of memory scattered through a maze. A slave born free. Trapped in a day, lost its way in poverty and graves, landmarks of moments stolen, now begs, plays reminiscent in moments frozen out, the film is rolling, the character is building, how was I struck, how'm I feeling? I've been numb, it felt dumb.

Kosal performed this piece on the night of the book launch for *Phnom Penh Noir* at the Foreign Correspondents' Club in Phnom Penh. His mother had come to hear her son perform for the first time. She'd never accepted his decision to be a poet, rapper, and singer. She wanted him to get a job as an electrician or plumber, to pursue a line of work that was solid and respectable and came with a regular paycheck. Everyone knew that poets came to nothing but poverty, grief, and an early grave. Like most Cambodians (and Thais) Kosal worshipped his mother, and her rejection of his ambitions cut him deep. It had been a wound that hadn't ever healed.

Kosal rapped his heart out that night at the FCCC. His mother, who'd flown in from the States for the event, sat in the front of the crowd in a new dress, her hair done up. When he'd finished performing, the two hundred plus guests responded with thunderous applause. He owned the audience that night. And he'd achieved that through his honest emotions. He reached deep into what had been broken, held captive in chains of the past, even chains of his own making, and his cry of the heart was the sound of those chains breaking. After the applause finally ended, we had our Hollywood ending after all. No yellow tab remaining in this script. Instead we had that rare genuine moment of a mother seeing her grown son for the first time and recognizing that he was someone special. Kosal put down the microphone and walked over to his mother, dropped to his knees, and embraced her. Were we watching an act of a mother's forgiveness or a son's redemption? I didn't know the answer that night and I still don't, but everyone in that room felt what passed between mother and son in those moments.

For the first time in his life, Kosal could see her pride in him, the son who'd been a gangster, an ex-con, and he'd been resurrected through his art. She fought back tears. The audience, which included a lot of old Asia hands who'd seen it all, had tears in their eyes. It would have taken a heart made of stone not to feel that mother's love for her son. It was one of those few moments that lodges itself permanently in the memory of witnesses—the sight of a mother and son reconciling, healing, unashamed to hug and cry, and able to move away from a past that had enslaved them.

Two years after that performance, Kosal starred in a documentary film about his life, titled *Cambodian Son*. Against the odds, he had used his raw talent, ambition, and determination to claw his way up from the bottom. He found in the years of bad memories a way to tell a story that only someone who had been through what he'd been through could tell. Episodic memory supplied all the worst experiences a man could suffer, and he'd fashioned them into poetry.

In 2011 and in later years, I ran into a number of other Cambodians who had been deported from the States after serving a prison sentence. They'd never gotten around to applying for US citizenship. Technically they remained aliens, and undesirable aliens were given the boot. Kosal represented the minority camp; he didn't hide his prison record and deportation. I found out that was unusual. Most men in circumstances like Kosal's kept their past in America to themselves. I remember a young photographer with lots of corporate clients. After his third gin and tonic he told me, in his large apartment filled with expensive furnishings, adjacent to a studio loaded with all the latest photography equipment, that he ran the risk of losing major clients if the word got around that he'd served time in America. I suspect a number of the savvy foreigners who employed him might have noticed that his English was too good, his manners too American, and few with those skills voluntarily returned to Cambodia to make their fortune.

If men like these had a facility with English and an understanding of the cultural norms of America, not learned in a refugee processing center but on American soil, they had great potential value in the job market and might get a respectable job with a foreign company. Admitting to being an ex-convict would spoil the CV. These men were a small part of the Cambodian diaspora who had involuntarily returned to a place they'd fled as children. They came back as adults, and they lacked neither the courage nor opportunity to break their chains.

The thing about memories is some of them are suitable for the arts, others for designing software, and yet others for running a company. Bad memories like the ones these ex-refugees have are a special category. Like a handicap they can leave the person who remembers them depressed, sad, alone, and helpless. When they were children, adults hurt them. No one was at their side when they most needed guidance. They made mistakes because no one taught them about mistakes. Later they found all those accumulated bad memories were difficult to keep walled up inside and even more difficult to share. They hadn't known any "safe space" as all of their spaces had been unsafe. They'd been robbed of the ability to trust. The worst of all thieves are the ones that steal a child's trust. Kosal and others like him had been abandoned at an age when a child needs to feel secure. They found only the street.

Bad memories put you at risk. Most people who have them keep them secret and drink to keep them below the surface. Kosal is the rare one who has taught himself a way of opening himself to the world. The night he performed at the launch of *Phnom Penh Noir*, he found something in his mother and two hundred guests that had eluded him for years, the most elusive of all gifts: love, admiration, and acceptance.

THIRTY-FOUR

In 2013, the year I had dinner with Dave Walker in Siem Reap, the Oscar for Best Picture went to *Argo*; the Nobel Prize for Literature was awarded to Alice Munro; the Grammy Award for Album of the Year was given for Mumford & Sons' *Babel*; Margaret Thatcher died.

When you want to describe motion through time and space, look to mathematical equations. You might disagree on the *why* of how something moved, but no matter your ideological perspective, you won't challenge the equation on the basis it is derived from fake numbers or that using whole number violates some sacred text. Humanity is united in its mathematical description of the *how* questions of the reality. There is no ultra-orthodox equivalent to $E = MC^2$ or the Dirac equation. No one kills a mathematician because of his use of zero. Mathematicians work through their equations writing, questioning, testing, and solving without any mullah pointing our theological errors. One reason for leaving mathematicians to their equations is the higher levels of the discipline can only be fathomed by other mathematicians. A theologian or politician wouldn't know where to start. The second reason mathematicians receive a free pass is they are only concerned with such matters as how things move, the forces of motion, and the nature of mass—realities that underlie our technological revolution.

But humans have no problem cutting each other's throats over the why questions that mathematics doesn't address. On most days I wish I'd had the talent to become a mathematician. It is a specialized language that only a few have any fluency in. Once those equations are translated into words, the conflicts, confrontations, and problems start multiplying. Beware of why questions in places like Cambodia and Thailand. Those questions expose cultural, class, and political fault lines.

I am not the first person, nor will I be the last, to ask some of the difficult why questions about the Khmer Rouge. When exploring other people's lives with a series of why questions, you are setting up a Venus flytrap.

Dave Walker liked asking the why type of question. Non-mathematicians who explore the why of things are also the group most likely to ignore the probabilities of someone being uncomfortable with such an inquiry and taking extreme measures to silence the questioner.

Not everyone in Cambodia is happy for the past to be remembered. People are killed because of what they remember. Other people are killed because they are asking people to open up their memories for a book or a film. David ("Dave") Walker, a friend, was a likely casualty because of his attempts to tap into the memories of the ex-Khmer Rouge.

Dave Walker had lived in Southeast Asia on and off over many years. He was an old hand. I met him through Richard Ehrlich, an American journalist, in Bangkok. That first encounter was in the early 1990s. The two of them hatched an idea (actually it had been Dave's idea) to collect letters that Dave and others had written for the freelance girls of the Thermae to send to their overseas boyfriends. Foreigners like Dave wrote the letters for the girls, who didn't have enough English to sign their name, usually asking for an emergency transfer of funds for some medical reason involving a brother, mother, water buffalo, or sometimes all three. The overseas boyfriend had no idea the letters had been ghost-written by a foreigner for the cost of a glass of Mekhong and Coke. This happened during the pre-Internet days, when people still exchanged letters via the post and long-distance calls cost a small fortune. I'd been published by White Lotus, a small press that specialized in reprints of out-of-print books written by long-dead authors. The books were academic, scholarly works about Southeast Asian culture, history, sociology, and anthropology. *A Killing Smile* had stuck out on the White Lotus list like a sore thumb on a concert pianist's right hand. But Dave and Richard sensed that my book might signal a new direction for the press.

Richard and Dave asked if I'd approach White Lotus's eccentric German-born publisher, Diethard Andre, to have a look at their book of bargirl letters. The idea was simple. If the publisher had been crazy enough to publish *A Killing Smile*, he might go for Dave and Richard's book. In 1992 White Lotus did bring out Dave and Richard's *Hello My Big Big Honey*, and the book became a smashing commercial success. It would sit in the catalogue beside titles such as Adolf Bastian's *Journey in Cambodia and Cochin-China (1864)* or John Anderson's *Mandalay to Momien*.

In the following years I occasionally ran into Dave Walker in Bangkok on the street, at the Foreign Correspondents' Club of Thailand, or in a bar. He always had a smile and a story. To make ends meet, Dave had briefly returned to Canada to drive a truck. He also worked as a crew member on movie projects that filmed in Southeast Asia. Dave was always drafting a new screenplay and hopeful of finding someone on a film set he was working on to read it. I wasn't surprised when I heard Dave had moved to Cambodia and rented a room in a Siem Reap guesthouse. In October 2013 I contacted Dave to let him know that my wife and I would be in town and asked if he'd like to have dinner.

I asked Dave to choose the restaurant. He picked his usual place, a back-alley open-air restaurant with concrete floors. He knew the staff there as well as the owners, whom I could see in the back with a gaggle of kids watching TV. Over dinner we caught up on mutual friends and his life in Cambodia. He had a local business partner, and the two of them had set up Animist Farm films. Dave's love was film. He told me about his efforts to shoot a documentary film project focused on the lives of ordinary Cambodians living in the countryside. David's idea was to pack up the camera gear and along with his partner and venture into the countryside. He set up his camera and microphone and recorded the stories of locals who had lived through the Khmer Rouge period. He interviewed them about their experiences, and they shared their memories with him. His production company ran on a shoestring budget, meaning he had no financing. Like his book with Richard, he'd gone into the field with his dreams believing that the money would turn up like a rainbow at the end of the day.

I asked Dave over dinner about his reception among the upcountry people he'd interviewed so far. Specifically I asked if he'd run into any resistance when he started digging up old memories. What I was really saying was, "Dave, what you're doing is crazy. You've got no one to watch your back. You need a powerful backer who can stand between you and someone who doesn't want foreigners digging into their past."

Dave shrugged off my concerns.

"My partner deals with that. They love and trust him. The villagers can't wait to talk in front of a camera. There's no need to wind them up. The stories pour out. There's no problem."

That was an old Thai sign-off when someone was pressed about a dangerous possibility: "No problem." There was always no problem, until there was.

Dave disappeared one day in January 2014 from his guesthouse, after tidying up his room so the two maids could go inside and clean it. Dave never returned that day. His body was found in a wooded area near Angkor Thom's Victory Gate. Clothed in black and a pair of gray sneakers, his body was in a badly decomposed state. There was an investigation, but the results were inclusive and no one was ever arrested. Dave's murder in early 2014 remains an unsolved mystery.

Others had done film documentaries based on the recollections of members of the Khmer Rouge. But those production teams had had support, money, and protection. Dave had had none of that, as I'd tried to tell him that day over dinner. He didn't want to hear that his ventures into the countryside ran more than a small probability of ending very badly. Dave told me he had already interviewed lots of the Old People who had been the most avid Khmer Rouge loyalists. Dave was good at getting others to talk into the camera. With his winning smile I could see him convincing an old uncle to talk about his time with the Khmer Rouge.

If you have visited any remote Cambodian villages, your first impression has likely been that time passes at a much slower pace there. What to us New People was ancient history remained the present for many of the Old People in the remote areas that had been Khmer Rouge strongholds. They had nothing when the Khmer Rouge came to power, and they had nothing now. They noticed little difference in their way of life. Left to their own devices, they stayed within the security of their areas, and sooner or later those old memories of the Khmer Rouge would die with the people who'd lived them. Asking the wrong individual about the Khmer Rouge would be like hitting a hornet's nest with a stick.

That night in Siem Reap Dave told me of his success in getting the villagers to open up about life under the Khmer Rouge. They had no problem sharing those stories with a foreigner on camera, he said. I knew it wouldn't take long before people in the area heard that one of the Old People had been sharing his memories of a forced-labor camp. Dave's questioning and filming would have excited suspicions. Old People talked to settle scores as much as to convey information. It was easy to rat out someone you didn't like with a story of how he murdered a family of New People with a hoe. Rumors fuel the paranoid fires of imagination. It would have been easy to misjudge Dave's motives and intentions. War crime tribunal trials were then under way in Phnom Penh. The locals would have been aware that some of the leaders were on trial. The fear of joining them in the dock would have been enough reason to mistrust Dave's work.

The New People came from a different tradition, one that valued and encouraged the expansion and updating of knowledge. In the Old People's world knowledge wasn't of that pedigree; knowledge was about crops, weather, trees, animals, and the like, or about who owed someone money or who had stolen a water buffalo. Some of that personal knowledge was guarded more like family secrets. It was easy to conclude that a person who shared local knowledge with an outsider was a traitor, and that the outsider was a spy.

Dave was no spy. He was an idealist, a romantic, and a filmmaker. But the cultural hurdle to jump between his world and their world was a high one.

I remember, that night in the restaurant around the corner from Dave's guesthouse, pointing out the danger of asking villagers about their experiences. Dave had been a British solider who had served in Northern Ireland. He had military training, he told me more than once. He figured that that background and training had given him enough courage to handle any confrontation. Dave may have been over-confident about the dangers he faced. No military training was going to protect an unconnected, meddling foreigner against those who'd likely had a hand in mass murder.

Dave had wandered into a closed, isolated community, thinking he was in control and would be safe. A lot of people have made the same mistake. It is easy to frame such communities as groups of simple people who are anti-knowledge, primitive, and backward. The reality is that the Old People draw their memories, wisdom, and worldview from a different body of knowledge. They view the New People's knowledge as a threat—filled with traps, lies, and heresies. The Khmer Rouge had emerged from their world. And their world was ringed with spirits, demons, and gods of the rivers and the forest, and they lived in families, alongside kin, and inside clans as they'd done for centuries. And they retained vivid memories of outsiders dropping bombs on their villages.

What was required for the safety of a filmmaker digging into the past inside Cambodia was celebrity status, connections, and money. Three years after dinner with Dave in Siem Reap, Angelina Jolie demonstrated that Dave's dream could be accomplished. All it took was a large budget, a big celebrity name attached, and solid political support. As a result, she was graced with the kind of immunity the feudalistic cultures extend to important people. Dave was never that important except to his friends and family.

Angelina Jolie's *First They Killed My Father* (2017) was shot in Cambodia and records the memories of Cambodians from the Khmer Rouge period. Dave's dream documentary was filmed by someone else.

Around the time that I'd written this chapter, I was moving office and came across an old file. I have the habit of keeping boarding passes, hotel receipts, brochures, newspaper clippings, name cards and the like. From that trip to Siem Reap, a folder yielded a thin *memento mori* of the trip. The first was the receipt showing what we had that dinner that night with David and his name card. We have no way of knowing what pieces of our past are locked in a file cabinet, a closet, a box or stored in the attic. Then one day we write about a person and a place, and that drainpipe from the past shoots us a message. You were there. Here's the evidence.

Restaurant receipt dated 13 October 2013 Siem Reap Cambodia

Dave Waker's name card 13 October 2013 Siem Reap Cambodia

THIRTY-FIVE

Cambodia taught me about the potential depths of fear and the seeds of a toxic hatred that men and women carry in their hearts. All it took was for a few people to nurture that seed, plumb those depths of fear, and fire up a movement. That meant someone or something to fear and hate. The New People fit the bill.

Genocide confirms our worst fears about humanity. There are powerful forces that wish to slaughter whole classes or groups of people. The Cambodian thug escorting the American basketball player around town that night and the Africans I'd seen outside the bar, defiantly holding their ground, suffered from the fear of social rejection. No one dies from such rejection, but we all fear it as if it were a social death sentence. Bopha had brushed against the true nature of physical fear when she witnessed the killing of a man in front of her. Kosal had feared many things—social and family rejection, physical fear of violence—but at the same time he'd found through poetry a way to break the chains that held him back, and learned through his art that the heaviest chains were those fashioned from fear. I'd seen fear on the faces of men shackled in T-3 prison and on the faces of those who'd passed through S-21 on their way to death and oblivion.

When I attended the war crimes tribunal, with a handful of Khmer Rouge leaders sitting behind a huge wall of glass, I noticed what was missing among the perpetrators. I felt the overwhelming sense of an absence. There was a quality of smugness about the accused, a sense that they thought we'd never know the true story. Memories are by nature incomplete, contradictory, and flawed, and these mass murderers were banking on the doubts and questions that memory's flaws invite. Not one of them looked afraid. Not one of them looked like a fired-up hatemonger. Instead they looked smug, bored, and defiant.

The accused in the dock were taken from the larger class of Khmer Rouge predators and plunderers. They had been just a few neurons in the Khmer Rouge brain that had devised and processed some of the policies. The genocide couldn't have been carried out without the co-operation of the Khmer cadre. The legion of true believers put those policies into action through widespread, systematic violence. There were many people who fell into this group. To go after them all risked civil unrest. The old men in the dock believed they were right, that they'd done nothing wrong, had harmed no one, and all the evidence to the contrary was false, lies spread by old enemies. Perhaps, when it came to confronting what they'd done, who'd said what, who'd ordered a policy, or who had executed it, they had fallen into a deep well of false memory where an alternative reality reigned.

I tried to imagine the fear that must have encircled the inhabitants of Phnom Penh on 17 April 1975, when the child soldiers entered the city. In *The Killing Fields* Roland Joffe had captured the haunting moments of terror among those whom the Khmer Rouge victors had crammed into the grounds of the American embassy.

There were deeper questions I wanted to understand. Exactly what was it in the mental operating system that distinguished the victims from their executioners? Was it more than having demonized the New People as 'Other', they no longer were human in the eyes of the executioners? The problem is that not all of them were educated, middle-class New People. And why had so many Cambodians joined the Khmer Rouge and participated in the genocide? Also, why had those in forced-labor camps voluntarily marched into the killing fields? It was the opposite of what I'd been taught about the fight-or-flight response triggered by fear. I haven't found the answers to these questions.

People often take a lifetime to cut through their fears. Only when we reach an advanced age will many of us look back and realize that a life lived in fear isn't much of a life to celebrate. The cultural anthropologist Ernest Becker wrote about how our fear of death is the source of our desire to transcend the body through religion or ideology; these belief systems don't so much cure fears with false promises of eternal life as tranquilize the fearful by injecting rituals and ceremonies. In the deep future, when human intelligence has achieved effective immortality, there will be no need for religion or ideology as there will be no fear-of-death consumers left to sell them to. We can't comprehend what will shape our memory to replace that overwhelming and powerful human fear. And yet, for all its personal and collective costs, the fear of death has been what has made us distinctly human over the entire course of our species' existence.

When I look at the current state of research on brains, I see how neural networks collect, channel, and store vast amounts of data that are filtered for threats. An event, person, or thing causes us to have an experience; it shows up in our heartbeat, respiration, and the electrical currents flowing under our skin. It's no surprise that Pol Pot, who was part of a long line of book-burning modern-knowledge haters, saw that the old knowledge was being destroyed in the name of scientific research and progress. The pursuit of knowledge harvested from big data was reducing ignorance even in his day and had slowly begun to diminish the shadow that fear cast over life and death. It is possible that understanding how the brain processes fear might someday lead to methods and techniques to minimize it. The truth is that above all we fear each other and the harm others can do to us. Our species' history is a testament to the violence we are capable of inflicting on each other. Over and over again we have given up our freedom to systems—and placed our faith in its doctrines—that have promised to increase our security. We have always wanted to live in a safe space at all costs. Our collective memories are curated reminders of how dangerous the world becomes once faith in authority evaporates. Once the crowd disperses, everyone is on their own.

Oliver Sacks documented a patient in his essay "The Lost Mariner," from *The Man Who Mistook His Wife for a Hat*, who through disease had lost his ability to form new memories and subsequently suffered amnesia that prevented him from gaining access to his old memories. Without new or old memories, his life disappeared and reappeared with each blink. No tangible connection linked his past to the present or bridged one thought to the next. The pipeline between the two was broken. The past became a guesswork game as he tried to remember what he'd been doing and where he'd been at any point in the past. For most of us, the loss of memory is gradual, almost unnoticed. We've all experienced that moment when a once-familiar name is on the tip of the tongue. The brain searches for a memory file but fails in its task. Try to return to your earliest memories and you'll find that the farther you go back, the more the people and places you find there blur as you enter a foggy valley of the brain. Spend long enough in this valley and you'll discover that something interesting happens in the process: you automatically fill in the blanks, without knowing you are doing it, using snippets culled from friends, family, movies, TV shows, books, essays, gossip, photographs. Before you know it, your brain has cut and pasted bits from multiple sources into a memory-scope you can use as a guide to your own lost past. We do this individually, and we also do it collectively as a society.

I accept that this process applies to me as well as everyone else. Jorge Luis Borges's "The Library of Babel" is a parable about an infinite library containing all possible combinations of meaning, memory and information. Borges takes us for a stroll through such a library to challenge our illusion that our memory belongs to us, that we own it—more than that, that it is part of who we are and it is a finite part of us. It is easy to forget that all of our memories gained through experience, learning, and socializing arise as mental re-enactments. But memories of objects are not themselves the real object in real time. Each is a mental copy of a copy of the original object as it appeared in the past. Facing the prospect that we are all lost mariners on a vast sea with no landmarks we can identify as our own disturbs our sense of self and uniqueness.

My memory of Cambodia appears to be "mine," when in fact it is pulled from many people, books, emails, letters, and conversations over nearly twenty-five years. I no longer remember where various bits originally came from when they entered my memory. I can't remember how, when, or where I learned that Phnom Penh is the capital of Cambodia. I know as a fact that it is, but who told me or how I came across that information, I can no longer recall.

A lot of our memory fits into this category—we find in our thinking an ignorance pothole and take out a mental shovel to fill it with extra information to eliminate doubts from the memory re-enactments. That, at least, seems a plausible explanation. Jorge Luis Borges wrote that "Doubt is one of the names of intelligence." Turn that Borges quote on its head and it is also true from the other direction, lack of doubt is one of the names of ignorance.

Pol Pot stood in a long line of memory strippers. He sought to murder his way to absolute power in a Cambodia populated by those whose memory of the past remained much as it always had been: basic, primitive, useful, limited, and local. Though Pol Pot could count such esoteric thinkers as the French lawyer Robespierre and the German author Marx among his guiding lights, when it came to Kampuchea, he and he alone would determine what kinds of memories were suitable for a new age beginning with the Year Zero. His way forward was to bury most of the modern world's memories along with the bodies that contained them in the killing fields. Like the Ancient Romans and the medieval church, he understood the importance of controlling the message. The precedent had been long established that a powerful priesthood wasn't possible in the absence of a singular, absolute, complete, and sacred memory—a sort of Borges infinite library before which he could stand guarding the door as chief librarian.

Humanity has a history of powerful players, from both the corporate and government worlds, actively working to extricate certain memories they find threatening or morally, politically, or spiritually abhorrent. I mentioned earlier how Emperor Theodosius in the fourth century had assisted in bringing about the collective amnesia of past religious beliefs and secular writings that had survived since Greek times. He burnt the books.

Between 350 and 1668 CE, Christian religious authorities in Europe carried out literary genocide, destroying and burning ancient Greek books of knowledge to prevent them from corrupting the minds of the faithful. In the eyes of the priesthood the ancient books threatened church doctrine and teachings.

The burning of books was highly effective. It was the only place where collective knowledge of the past could be found. Once the Greek texts had been destroyed, there was no knowledge left to contradict the church dogma. To eliminate doubt was the church's ultimate goal. Alternative voices, especially the educated ones, carried those doubts and contrary explanations into the public memory. The first time the word "freethinker" is known to have appeared in English was 1692. That was around the time when the book-burning era was closing and the church was losing its power to close down or control the printing presses. When an old civilization goes extinct, the people who once were part of it forget, as does the next generation and the one after that, until no one who remembers any experience of its institutions, culture, or sacred values is left alive.

Memory cleansing, like ethnic cleansing, combines fear, hatred, and hubris, using them as brooms to sweep out the old memories. As one set of beliefs replaces another, the new belief system depends on a collective forgetting so that a different order of thoughts can be established in the minds of the people. There can be no conquest without defeating and destroying old memories of the past that conflict with the new belief system. Pol Pot understood the dangers of Democritus, Copernicus, Darwin, and many others as existential threats in the memory competition business. No supernatural or utopian belief system has survived contact with such thinkers. Cultures have their cherished memories to preserve. The cost of their preservation is written in accounts of torture chambers, death camps, and mass graves. The shakier the foundation of the belief system, the more violent is the official reaction to evidence that contradicts the beliefs, or worse, to the description of a more coherent, testable, and repeatable method to describe reality.

Our memories are the center of our personal universe. A society's collective memories are the bonds that tie people together in a common culture. The history of Cambodia shows the consequences of destroying the old bonds through violence and force. For almost twenty-five years I've followed the characters, the policies, the justifications, the rationales, the camps, the deportations, the suffering, and the hardship that controlling past memory entails. Pol Pot's regime used brutal and ruthless means because they believed the end goal of new memories justified them.

Angkor Wat and the temples surrounding it provide an example of a memory collapse that followed the end of a civilization. Since the French explorer Henri Mouhot reached Angkor Wat in January 1860, the myth has continued that this complex of temples had been forgotten by the world for hundreds of years prior to that. We were led to believe by Henri Mouhot that Angkor Wat had disappeared from our general world memory. But others—a French missionary, a Portuguese monk, and a Portuguese trader—had reported on their visits to Angkor Wat before Mouhot. The Cambodians who lived in the surrounding area certainly possessed knowledge about its existence. But their voices had no way to reach the outside world. They'd been cut adrift because they had lost the means of communicating their presence.

Debunking legends is a difficult business. Many chose to believe that Angkor Wat had been long forgotten by the time it was rediscovered by Mouhot. The reality is that Mouhot's so-called discovery was a matter of good timing, literary skill, and good public relations that plugged into the larger world communication grid. Of course he also had good luck on his side. Henri Mouhot's writings restored to our pool of common knowledge that there were magnificent ancient ruins of a civilization around Angkor Wat, a civilization that had come to an end in the early fifteenth century. He seemed to have pulled a rabbit out of a hat. An entire civilization that had vanished had reappeared. Henri Mouhot had given us the gift of remembering what we'd collectively forgotten or failed to discover on our personal exploration through the infinite Library of Babel.

THIRTY-SIX

M any examples exist of the re-emergence of long-forgotten places or ideas. Democritus had written about the "atom" as the basic building block of reality. He's been described as the father of modern science. We know of Democritus only through the writings of others; his own writings didn't survive the great burnings of the Middle Ages. Not until the age of the printing press was Democritus rediscovered like a "lost" Angkor Wat. That rediscovery opened up new avenues for exploration as his tools in mathematics, geometry, and the nature of the knowledge of truth equipped a new generation, separated from its predecessors by nearly a thousand years, to restart the inquiry into heretical ideas about reality inside a materialist universe.

We retain the same mental operating system that our ancestors had thousands of years ago. At present it is not upgradable. We are in the midst of an information, knowledge, and technological revolution. The past teaches us that when such transformation happens, the old system is gradually erased from collective memory as new content is laid down, overwriting the old. No one today directly remembers European feudalism or the early Industrial Age of steam. Those memories are semantic and, like the products of taxidermy, lifeless and frozen in time and space. The possibility of bringing the dead past to life again is the dream of civilization destroyers and memory rewriters. What they deliver is inevitably a Frankenstein's monster. It becomes a political franchise manufacturing pre-programmed golems sent out to live unrecognized among us.

It may turn out that we learn that our brains are too limited by their biological structure to understand the scope of violence in the universe. All of our fears are homegrown, local, and immediate. In terms of the rest of the universe, we are all Pol Pot's Old People clinging to ways of thinking evolved from a specific accident of our origins in Africa. Not unlike Henri Mouhot, I've written a book about what many others more knowledgeable already know about Cambodia, its people, history, and culture. I don't claim any special discovery in this memory exploration. My set of memories is incomplete, and some of them may prove to be false or fabricated in ways I don't fully appreciate.

Anyone in the distant future who sits in judgment over this manifesto will likely have a set of memories that comes equipped with a richer, deeper understanding of how the human brain naturally processes memory. These are the early days of neuro-scientific research. Once that memory-consciousness-subjectivity puzzle is unraveled, we may appear to those intelligent beings in the future as a curious variation of Oliver Sacks's *Lost Mariner*, but with one major difference—our memories won't have been disabled by brain disease. We'll be seen as refusing to accept the verdict that such brains could only take us so far.

In the digital age that we're now beginning, erasing the past will be more difficult. It's not only in books; it's in hundreds of millions of computers around the world. Nothing, in theory, can be lost again, though finding it may take effort and time. That too will change as new processes make it easier to process and remember a volume of information way beyond our current ability.

Pol Pot's legacy shows that with concentrating murder and violence to destroy the memory of the past, our collective memory is too resilient and recovers from attempted acts of mass destruction. The time has passed when a people can be confined to a single controlled memory room closed off from the rest of the world. Memory from the outside leaks in and sealing the cracks that let in the light is doomed to failure. The era of mass memory management has left a rearguard of censorship in many countries, and like the Dutch boy with his finger in the dike, it is just a matter of time before an overflow of information washes away the barriers.

Our current manner of controlled, manipulated, selective remembering will be assigned to the category of primate limitations. We will witness a frightened amazement as the realization that our understanding of our memory of the world was only a roughly sketched map of the world and we'll find ourselves back in a world no longer legible to us, in fact back where we started—with our memory gates fragile, malleable, and unstable. We will no longer know who or what to believe, and memory ghettos will gather the faithful and true believers. They will circle the wagons. History documents this very human response to threats against existing beliefs, institutions, and social relationships. Upheaval on the scale that happened during the 1970s in Cambodia contradicts the Whig view of history as following an upward line toward more progress and development.

Cambodia has taught me many lessons about the nature of memory, but our science of memory still hasn't solved the mystery of how it works. As long as that mystery remains, we can take some small comfort that our memories matter to our sense of self and to our belongingness to a culture and a country. We recall our past and the places, people, and events in it through re-enactments scripted from analog and digital information encoded in our brains. Memory is our personal documentary archive. But for us our memory is not an archive or a film; it's real, tangible, with images, sounds, scents, and feelings. We persist in the belief that we can relive what we've experienced and that we can learn from experiences in the past. Without that belief we lose causality. And that would do more damage than losing our gods.

The fact is that outside forces in government and the corporate world share an interest in editing our memories. They don't ask our permission. We are unaware that editing is happening. The intention is to align memories—because when we agree on what happened, we avoid conflict over responsibility for the results. Memory is politicized, and the means of carrying out memory "transplants" or "wipes" were likely more available in the past. Burn all of the books. Kill all of the intellectuals. None of that has worked over the long term. But we are at the start of a new technological era in which machines will encode our memories from birth. At first the results the new processes of memory formation and alteration will be uneven and controversial, and will excite our suspicions. But the learning curve will be faster than the ability of the negative pushback forces to marshal their protest. Aldous Huxley's *Brave New World* was a prescient insight into what happens when we cross over the new memory frontier. With each new technological breakthrough we inch closer to that frontier.

I've used my memory records, both from my own experience and from my research, to paint a miniature of a time and place while observing how that time and place are processed in our memory. Memory is a danger zone.

It is fallible. Buffeted by limited resources, incomplete information, and opinions based on anecdotes. Memory is more like a dream where we believe we witness the truth and that our eyes are wide open. We live at a time when patriots and ultranationalists in many places are preparing to use violence to preserve their versions of the truth. Cambodia, if they care to examine its history, shows the risks of taking that dreamer's road.

At the beginning of this book I raised a metaphysical question about whether our memory, individually or collectively, has any real tangible meaning in the universe. I end the book with the admission that I don't know. No one does. That means we have no choice but to accept that there is no right answer and we are left to speculate. That said, we pay a high emotional price for signing on to the belief that our memories have no meaning. Even if that is ultimately true, we need the illusion of meaning and purpose. We will cling to our memories to the very end.

The artists, writers, thinkers, philosophers and teachers have been assigned the role of memory transmitters; they perform the service of mandala keepers, who leave their generations offerings before a gateway to greater understanding. José Saramago in his novel *Blindness* wrote: "The difficult thing isn't living with other people, it's understanding them." Understanding ourselves must precede understanding others, and that is the most difficult of the tasks that falls to the memory transmitters.

We can't choose our time. Time has chosen us and that choice is filled with contradictions and paradoxes we must endure. William Shakespeare captured the cat and mouse nature of the timing game that is played on us. "When I got enough confidence, the stage was gone. When I was sure of losing, I won. When I needed people the most, they left me. When I learnt to dry my tears, I found a shoulder to cry on. And when I mastered the art of hating, somebody started loving me."

To believe that my memory has no real meaning in the universe requires me to discard a core vanity: that my and your memory matters somehow to the universe. I end this memory manifesto with an observation, actually more of a prediction, that letting go of our central role of memory in our universe will be the last vanity we will repudiate. We've already lost our gods. Without the spiritual possibility, we confront head on our fear of death as the ultimate act of memory encryption. Without the special place we assign to memory, posterity—that invisible desire to live on— becomes a ghostly phantom of our imagination. Gabriel García Márquez expressed the futility of understanding our human condition in *Love in the Time of Cholera*, "Wisdom comes to us when it can no longer do any good."

To conclude that memory is meaningless on the cosmic scale is more terrifying than governments and corporations that have devoted vast resources to creating false memories. The best we can hope for is to ignore the larger metaphysical problem and, like my character named Sam in "Reunion," seek comfort, security, and diversions as the most sensible plan to complete our time. From an embrace to a kiss, to an offered hand to someone who needs us, to feel the wind at our backs as we sail forward reading the poetry in the stars, smelling the sea air, and watching the sun setting over a river—these are our life experiences. They are who we are to ourselves. And we still live in a time when it is possible to distract ourselves from weighing the implication that nothing about us or that happens to us ultimately is memorable, yet we are natural born solipsist when it comes to memory. We can't help ourselves from prostrating in front of our personal memory altar.

If time and space are the universe's monorail, what is traveling along that entangled rail, if not memory? At this level forgetting a memory isn't permitted by the system any more than our self-contained universe can lose information. It's all there waiting to be decoded and sent down the line. We are in one carriage for a brief time and cover a short space, and like all particles seem to disappear but are merely transformed to another state. Those particles were always a kind of story narrating the approximations of the field underneath.

In the blink of the cosmic eye, those who come after us will be better equipped to translate our memory flashes as signals in a much grander network of synapses firing an infinite set of the neurons woven into space-time. Those who will come after us will have a better understanding of what Jorge Luis Borges meant when he wrote *In Praise of Darkness*, "We are our memory, we are that chimerical museum of shifting shapes, that pile of broken mirrors." For us we will continue to push on through the heaps of broken mirrors dreaming of our reflection and surprised by what we see.

Christopher G. Moore is a Canadian novelist and essayist who lives in Bangkok. He has written 27 novels, including the award-winning Vincent Calvino series and the Land of Smiles Trilogy. The German edition of his third Vincent Calvino novel, *Zero Hour in Phnom Penh*, won the German Critics Award (Deutsche Krimi Preis) for International Crime Fiction in 2004 and the Spanish edition of the same novel won the Premier Special Director's Book Award Semana Negra (Spain) in 2007. The second Calvino novel, *Asia Hand*, won the Shamus Award for Best Original Paperback in 2011.

CPSIA information can be obtained
at www.ICGtesting.com
Printed in the USA
LVOW05s2256220817
546022LV00011B/133/P